TOP 10 ANDALUCÍA AND THE COSTA DEL SOL

CONTENTS

4 Introducing Andalucía and the Costa del Sol

18 Top 10 Highlights

46

Top 10 of Everything

86

Area by Area

136

Streetsmart

ANDALUCÍA AND THE COSTA DEL SOL

INTRODUCING

A beautiful stretch of coastline in Nerja

WELCOME TO

ANDALUCÍA AND COSTA DEL SOL

Sun-drenched and steeped in history, Andalucía is the heart and soul of Spain, from the snow-dusted peaks of the Sierra Nevada to the glistening Mediterranean shoreline. With Top 10 Andalucía and the Costa del Sol you'll enjoy the very best the region has to offer.

In the words of the famous Andalucían poet Federico García Lorca, "Andalucía is not a place you visit, it is a place that stays with you forever". And he might just be right. Few places offer such a vivid blend of history, culture and natural beauty. Andalucía is where Europe meets North Africa in a cultural fusion. It's the birthplace of flamenco and tapas, and home to

The iconic Plaza de España in Seville

three of Spain's most iconic cities: Seville, where orange blossoms scent the air; Granada, crowned by the majestic Alhambra; and Córdoba, home to the grand Mezquita and historic Jewish quarter. Sure, exploring every inch of those cities could take a lifetime, but there's plenty more to discover here.

Venture south to the Costa del Sol and the mood softens to sun-soaked leisure. Stretching along the Mediterranean, this coastline is famed for its golden beaches and glamorous resorts like Marbella, famed for its bustling nightlife, or the more laid-back Nerja, a former fishing village turned beach town, with stretching sea views. In the region's rugged mountain terrain, meanwhile, you'll find Spain's iconic *pueblos blancos*, also known as the white hilltop towns. There's Ronda, dramatically located on the edge of a canyon; Zahara de la Sierra, perched atop a mountain; and, further west, Grazalema, known for its lush trails and striking limestone cliffs.

So, where to start? With Top 10 Andalucía and the Costa del Sol, of course. This pocket-sized guide gets to the heart of the region with simple lists of 10, expert local knowledge and comprehensive maps, helping you turn an ordinary trip into an extraordinary one.

THE STORY OF ANDALUCÍA AND COSTA DEL SOL

With its rich and diverse history, shaped by multiple civilizations over thousands of years, Andalucía has played a vital role in the cultural, political and economic life of the Iberian Peninsula. Here's the story of how it came to be.

An illustration of Menga dolmen, an ancient megalithic site

Prehistoric Beginnings

The history of Andalucía begins in prehistoric times, with evidence of early human settlement in the Palaeolithic period, notably the cave paintings of the Cueva de la Pileta and Cuevas de Nerja, which date back over 30,000 years. As societies developed, the indigenous Iberians left remarkable megalithic structures such as the Dolmens of Antequera, highlighting their early shared social and religious practices.

One of the earliest known civilizations, the Tartessos flourished between the 9th and 6th centuries BCE. Located in what is now western Andalucía, they developed a sophisticated society based on agriculture, metallurgy and trade. They were especially known for their exploitation of mineral resources like gold, silver and tin. Their contact with Eastern Mediterranean traders, particularly the Phoenicians, influenced Tartessian culture, shaping aspects of writing, religion and artistic expression.

The seafaring Phoenicians established trading posts along the Andalucían coast, most notably founding Gadir (modern-day Cádiz) around 1104 BCE, making it one of the oldest continuously inhabited cities in Europe. This marked the beginning of extensive trade

networks and cultural exchange. Over time, the Carthaginians (descendants of Phoenician settlers in North Africa) expanded their influence in southern Iberia. However, their dominance came to an end with Rome's victory in the Punic Wars, 264–146 BCE.

Roman Hispania

After the defeat of Carthage in the Second Punic War, 218–201 BCE, the Romans incorporated the region into their empire, naming it Hispania Baetica. Andalucía quickly became a prosperous province due to its fertile lands and strategic ports, and urban centres flourished, especially Itálica, located near present-day Santipoce in the province of Sevilla. Founded in 206 BCE, Itálica was notable as the birthplace of emperors Trajan and Hadrian. The city boasted impressive Roman infrastructure, including paved roads and one of the largest amphitheatres in Hispania. Roman law, Latin language, urban planning and monumental architectural style left an enduring legacy in Andalucía despite the Roman's eventual decline.

Moorish Era

In 711 CE, Muslim forces from North Africa crossed the narrow Strait of Gibraltar and began the conquest of the Iberian Peninsula, establishing the territory known as Al-Andalus. For over 700 years, Andalucía flourished under Muslim rule, becoming a centre of learning and innovation. Cities like Córdoba, Seville and Granada were known for their impressive mosques, advanced irrigation systems and a vibrant cultural life where Muslim, Jewish and Christian communities at times coexisted and contributed to developments in science, medicine and philosophy.

A 19th-century engraving of Roman and Carthaginian fleets

Moments in History

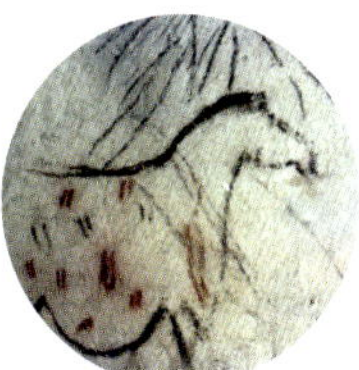

c 30,000 BCE
Cave paintings are created in the Cueva de la Pileta and Cuevas de Nerja, evidence of prehistoric human presence.

c 1104 BCE
The Phoenicians found Gadir (modern Cádiz), establishing a key Mediterranean trading post.

c 900 BCE
The Tartessos civilization thrives in western Andalucía, developing a sophisticated society based on agriculture, metallurgy and trade.

206 BCE
The Romans found Itálica near Seville, later the birthplace of emperors Trajan and Hadrian.

711 CE
Muslim forces invade the Iberian Peninsula, establishing Al-Andalus and shaping Andalucían culture.

1492
Granada surrenders to the Catholic Monarchs, and Christopher Columbus begins exploration of the Americas.

1812
The Spanish Constitution is drafted, a landmark in European liberal history.

1936
The Spanish Civil War begins, sparking intense conflict throughout Andalucía, as rival forces vie for control across the region.

1959
Tourism booms in the Costa del Sol, with the development of resorts and improved transport links.

1981
Andalucía gains autonomy through a referendum, officially becoming an autonomous community of Spain.

2023
Andalucía becomes Europe's leading producer of solar energy, marking a new era in green energy leadership.

Columbus bidding farewell to Isabel and Fernando in 1942

The Reconquista and Age of Exploration

From the 11th century onwards, Muslim control fragmented into smaller kingdoms, making the region more vulnerable to advancing Christian kingdoms from the north. This gradual military and political campaign, known as the *Reconquista*, culminated in 1492 with the fall of Granada to the Catholic Monarchs. This marked the end of Muslim rule in Spain and the beginning of a unified Christian kingdom under Spain's Fernando II and Isabel I.

During the ensuing years, conquistadors travelled to Central and South America, founding colonies for the Spanish Crown and returning with vast wealth – at the cost of the Indigenous population. In 1503, the Casa de la Contratación (House of Trade) was established in Seville, handing the city a monopoly on trade with the Americas. The city flourished as a result. Exquisite buildings were constructed and people flocked to this new cultural hub. But it wasn't to last. As the country's principal port, Seville suffered greatly during ruinous wars with France and the Low Countries, and when the Río Guadalquivir silted up in the 18th century, the trading monopoly passed to Cádiz.

From the 18th century onwards, Andalucía experienced profound political, social and economic transformations. The decline of transatlantic trade and shifts in global commerce weakened local agriculture and sparked unrest, laying the groundwork for upheavals in the 19th century.

A Country at War

After the War of Spanish Succession (1701–1714), the Bourbon dynasty rose to power, drawing Spain into the orbit of French politics. This alliance led to involvement in the Napoleonic Wars. In 1808, Napoleon invaded Spain and placed his brother on the throne, triggering the Peninsular War. Cities like Cádiz became centres of resistance and liberal thought. In 1812, Cádiz hosted the drafting of Spain's first constitution, one of the earliest in Europe.

Following Napoleon's defeat and the restoration of the Spanish monarchy, Andalucía entered a period of industrialization, with hubs like Huelva and Málaga experiencing significant growth. For the most part, however, the region remained economically stagnant, and large swathes of the countryside saw little development. The loss of Spain's American colonies by the century's end further deepened economic hardship, and at the turn of the 20th century, widespread rural poverty and feudal land ownership stoked social discontent. Protests and worker movements grew, contributing to political instability and the outbreak of the Spanish Civil War in 1936. General Francisco Franco's Nationalist forces quickly took control of Andalucía, establishing it as a base for the wider campaign. Under Franco's dictatorship (1939–1975), repression was severe – tens of thousands were executed, and democratic freedoms were crushed.

Andalucía Today

After Franco's death, Spain transitioned peacefully to democracy. King Juan Carlos I rejected absolute power and embraced constitutional monarchy. The 1980s brought renewed optimism, too: in 1981, Andalucía achieved autonomy by referendum, with Seville becoming its capital, and in 1986 Spain joined the European Economic Community. As a result Andalucía modernized rapidly, fuelled by tourism and European Union investment.

Although the 2008 global financial crisis hit hard, today Andalucía is one of Europe's top holiday destinations, attracting millions to iconic cities like Seville, Granada and Córdoba every year. The region works hard to honour its rich and diverse cultural heritage while shaping a vibrant, forward-looking future – here, sustainable practices and tech start-ups are just as important as flamenco and UNESCO World Heritage Sites.

Calle Sierpes in Seville, famed for its shopping and charm

TOP 10 EXPERIENCES

Planning the perfect trip to Andalucía and the Costa del Sol? Whether you're visiting for the first time or revisiting, here are some things you simply shouldn't miss out on. To make the most of your time – and to enjoy the very best this region has to offer – be sure to add these experiences to your list.

1 Admire the architecture

Andalucía's architecture invites you to explore its rich history first-hand. Marvel at modern landmarks like Seville's Metropol Parasol *(p93)* or lose yourself in the Roman ruins of Itálica *(p101)*. The region's unique blend of old and new tells a story in every stone, tile and arch.

2 Walk the Caminito del Rey

The Caminito del Rey is an unforgettable adventure along narrow pathways set in the steep rock face of El Chorro Gorge *(p112)*. Once known as the world's most dangerous hike, it has been fully restored for safety while preserving its thrilling edge and stunning views of Andalucía's rugged natural beauty.

3 Indulge in a hammam experience

Step back in time to the era of Al-Andalus with a visit to one of Andalucía's immersive hammams *(p128)*. Relax in warm pools and enjoy soothing massages and aromatic steam. It's just the ticket after a busy day of sightseeing.

4 Enjoy a tapas tour

Tapas in Andalucía is a feast for the senses and a true cultural delight, and what better way to experience it than on a tapas tour. Wander through lively streets, sampling bite-sized local specialities. Try delights such as crispy calamari, rich *arroz a la marinera* or refreshing gazpacho *(p78)*.

5 Taste delicious sherry

Wine lovers and history buffs alike will delight in exploring Andalucía's rich sherry heritage in Jerez de la Frontera. Tour historic bodegas *(p80)*, discover the unique *solera* ageing process and savor an array of wines, from the crisp, dry *fino* to the sweet Pedro Ximénez.

6 Immerse yourself in flamenco

Flamenco is at the heart of Andalucían culture. Catch a captivating live performance in Seville, Granada or Málaga, or head to a local *peña* for a more intimate experience performed by passionate local artists *(p95)*.

7 Visit los pueblos blancos

Nestled in the scenic hills of Cádiz and Málaga, the region's "white villages" *(p109)* are a collection of charming towns known for whitewashed houses, cobbled streets and stunning views. Ronda *(p36)*, Grazalema *(p112)* and Zahara de la Sierra *(p61)* are just a few.

8 Catch the waves

The best places to hit the waves are along the coast where the Mediterranean meets the Atlantic, particularly Cádiz *(p34)* and Huelva *(p99)*. Tarifa *(p68)* is renowned for its perfectly windy conditions, though excellent options extend along the entire coast.

9 Explore caves and caverns

Andalucía is home to a stunning array of prehistoric caves and caverns, offering a glimpse into ancient geological and human history. Highlights include the Cuevas de Nerja *(p76)* and the Gruta de las Maravillas *(p100)*, famed for their otherworldly beauty.

10 Gaze at the night sky

Low levels of light pollution, clear night skies and rugged mountain ranges make Andalucía a stargazer's paradise. In Almería, the Tabernas Desert and Cabo de Gata-Níjar Natural Park *(p69)* offer some of the region's most spectacular night skies.

ITINERARIES

Exploring Moorish monuments, tucking into delicious tapas or wandering whitewashed villages: there's a lot to see and do in Andalucía. With places to eat, drink or simply take in the view, these itineraries offer ways to spend 4 or 7 days in the region.

4 DAYS

Day 1

Begin your Andalucían adventure in the heart of Seville with the awe-inspiring Seville Cathedral *(p26)*, the largest Gothic cathedral in the world. Opt for the morning rooftop tour if available, as it offers sweeping panoramic views. After exploring the interior and climbing the Giralda tower, wander into the winding alleys of the city's former Jewish quarter, Barrio Santa Cruz. Pause for lunch at Casa Plácido *(p97)*, known for its traditional Andalucían flavours. Later, head to Plaza de España *(p91)*, Seville's grand plaza built for the 1929 Ibero-American Expo. Stroll the tiled bridges and canals before continuing into Parque de María Luisa *(p93)*, where relaxing fountains invite a leisurely pause. As dusk settles, savour some tapas at Lobo López *(p97)* and cap the night with a show at Teatro Flamenco Sevilla *(p95)*.

Boating on the canal that surrounds the Plaza de España

DRINK

After the light show at Las Setas, head to Premier Sherry Cocktail Bar *(p96)*, where staff share their knowledge of sherry. Explore the tasting menu or enjoy a creative sherry-based cocktail that reimagines this Andalucían classic.

Day 2

Start the day with a short bus ride to the Roman ruins of Itálica *(p101)* and explore its vast amphitheatre and ancient streets. For lunch, settle in at La Caseta De Antonio *(p101)* in nearby Santiponce for a paella that blends tradition with local flair. Back in Seville, step into the majestic Real Alcázar *(p28)*, a dazzling example of Mudéjar architecture. As evening approaches, dine at Pan y Circo, a refined space serving Andalucían produce with a modern twist. When night falls, head to Las Setas *(p93)* for the light show, a futuristic contrast to the city's ancient heart.

Day 3

Catch an early train to Córdoba, just 40 minutes from Seville, and dive into the city's rich heritage. Start with the

Mezquita *(p32)*, a mosque-turned-cathedral filled with rows of red-and-white striped arches. From there, stroll the flower-lined streets of the Jewish quarter and visit the historic synagogue *(p49)*, which dates back to 1315. For lunch try riverside dining at the charmingly traditional Horno San Luis *(p135)*. Spend the afternoon immersed in craftsmanship at Plata Con Alma Ana Martínez, where skilled artisans continue Córdoba's legacy of filigree jewellery. Then wander the peaceful gardens of the Alcázar de los Reyes Cristianos *(p63)* before returning to Seville for a relaxed dinner at Mariatrifulca *(p97)*.

Day 4

Spend your morning immersed in art at the Museo de Bellas Artes *(p90)*, where masterpieces by Spanish painters like Murillo and Velázquez await. After taking it all in, treat yourself to elegant fine dining at Taberna del Alabardero *(p97)*, known for its refined cuisine and charming atmosphere. After lunch, take a riverside stroll along Paseo Alcalde Marqués de Contadero *(p93)* and unwind in the beautiful Jardines de Murillo *(p93)*. For dinner, enjoy tapas at Casa Morales *(p96)* before rooftop cocktails at Pura Vida Terraza *(p96)*.

7 DAYS

Day 1

Start your journey in Granada with a visit to the iconic Alhambra *(p22)*, a masterpiece of Moorish architecture. Book tickets in advance to explore its intricate palaces and tranquil gardens. From there, wander uphill to the Albaicín *(p124)*, the city's ancient Moorish quarter. Take in views of the Alhambra from the Mirador de San Nicolás, stop for tea in a traditional *tetería* and soak up the atmosphere. Make time for the cave homes of Sacromonte before ending the day at the tranquil Hammam Al Ándalus baths *(hammamalandalus.com)*. For dinner, head to the lively Bib-Rambla square in the centre of Granada for Andalucían tapas under twinkling lights.

Day 2

Drive an hour and a half east through scenic desert landscapes to Mini Hollywood *(p77)*, an old Western film set near Tabernas that doubles as a unique theme park. Explore its frontier-style saloons and cowboy re-enactments before lunching in a local café. Continue your journey south to the coastal city of Almería *(p122)* to visit its grand Alcazaba *(p53)*, a 10th-century fortress with panoramic views. Dive into local history

Re-created Western town in Almería's Mini Hollywood

at the Museo de Almería, then head to Plaza de la Constitución for dinner at Restaurante Cuatro Hojas *(Plaza de la Constitución 3)*, where creative chefs bring modern flair to regional flavours.

Day 3

Follow the coast south to Playa de San José *(p68)*. Hire a paddleboard or snorkel and spend the day in the sea or lounging on the beach. Lunch on fresh seafood at a beachfront restaurant and dine come evening at Mirador del Faro *(C/la Morra 4b)*, perched just above the coastline. When night falls, stargaze at the peaceful Playa de los Genoveses within the Cabo de Gata *(p66)*.

Day 4

Head west to Málaga, enjoying a picturesque drive through the whitewashed

> **VIEW**
> Málaga's Alcazaba *(p53)* terraces overlook the cathedral, port and beaches. Morning light highlights the architecture, while sunsets cast a warm glow, offering captivating views at any time.

villages of the Costa Tropical. Pause in Frigiliana to admire cobbled lanes and artisan shops, then continue to Nerja to explore its famous caves *(p76)* and hidden coves. For lunch try traditional local specialities such as *salmorejo* or fried fish. Then it's the final push to Málaga, and a visit to the Museo Picasso Málaga *(p56)* in the artist's birthplace. After, take in sweeping views of the coast from the city's Alcazaba *(p53)*. End the day with modern tapas at Viznaga *(C/ Luis de Velázquez 7)*, followed by a flamenco show at Teatro Flamenco Málaga *(p55)*.

Day 5

Leave the coast and venture inland towards Ronda *(p36)*. Stop in Carratraca, a small village known for its Roman-era thermal springs and the historic Trinidad Grund Palace. When you arrive in Ronda, enjoy a delicious lunch at Restaurante Tropicana *(p117)*, where you'll find a variety of Mediterranean and globally influenced dishes. To kick off the afternoon, visit Plaza de Toros bullring *(p37)* to learn about the complex history of bullfighting, before crossing the Puente Nuevo bridge and exploring La Casa del Rey Moro *(p36)*. Wander the old town's narrow streets for hidden viewpoints and timeless charm. Later, stop by Mondragón Palace Museum *(p36)*, which also has beautiful gardens and courtyards. For dinner, reserve a table on the terrace at Arrabal *(C/ Tenorio 12)*, where views of Ronda's gorge are as stunning as the food.

Ornate arches at Seville's La Casa de Pilatos

Day 6

Travel an hour and a half west to Jerez *(p110)*, a city known for its equestrian traditions and sherry. Tour the Alcázar and if timing allows, catch the "Dancing Horses" at the Royal Andausian School of Equestrian Art. Wander the historic centre, shop artisan goods, and stop for lunch at a local taberna for traditional dishes like *rabo de toro* (oxtail stew) or *flamenquín* (breaded pork or chicken). In the afternoon, visit a local bodega for a guided sherry tasting *(p80)*, then enjoy tapas at Bar Juanito *(p117)*.

Day 7

End your trip in Seville *(p88)*, Andalucía's vibrant capital. Begin with the elegant Casa de Pilatos *(p89)*, then lose yourself in the flower-filled lanes of Barrio Santa Cruz. Pause for lunch at Casa La Viuda *(p97)*, for traditional dishes in a charming setting. Later, ascend the undulating catwalks of Metropol Parasol *(p93)* for panoramic city views, and visit the ornate Casa de la Condesa de Lebrija *(p92)*. Wrap up your journey with a sunset dinner cruise on the Guadalquivir River. Esturión Tours *(esturiontours.com)* offers several scenic options.

TOP 10 HIGHLIGHTS

Detail of the Alhambra's Patio de los Leones, Granada

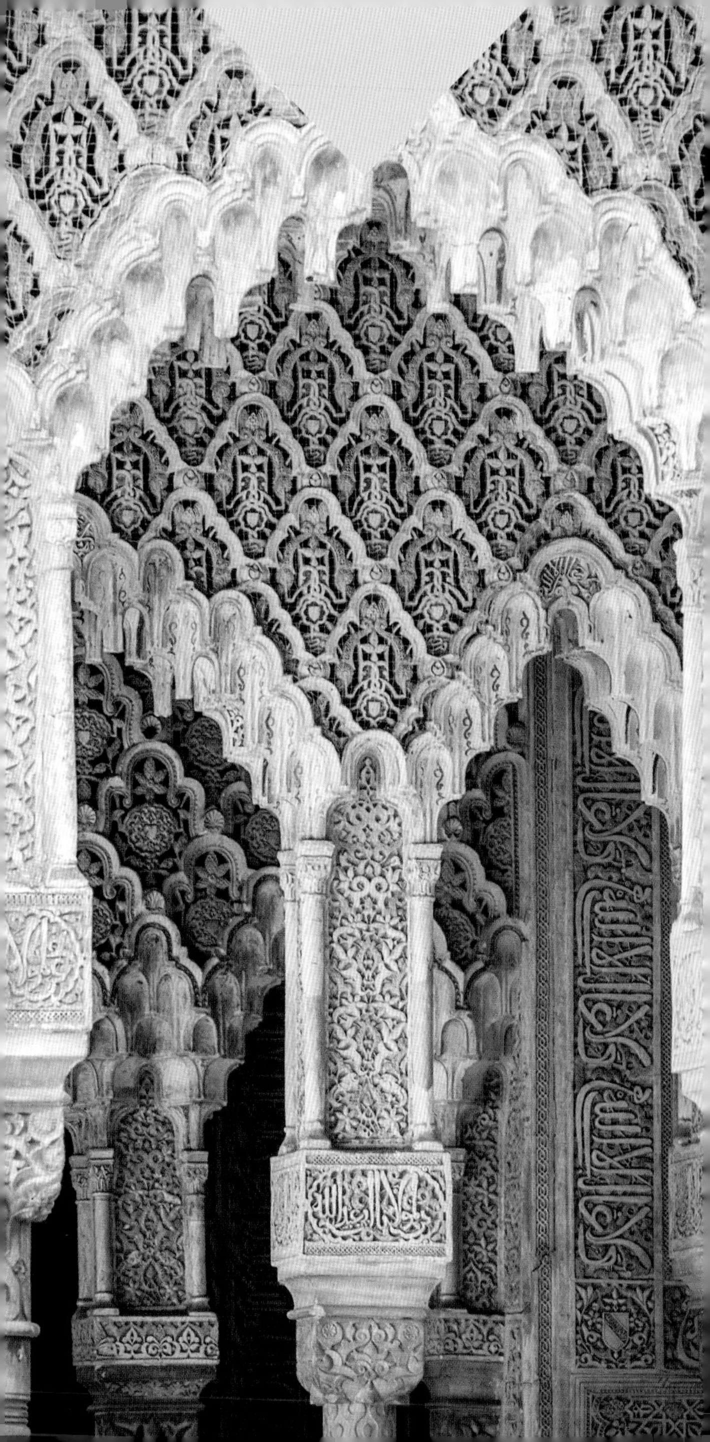

EXPLORE THE HIGHLIGHTS

There are some sights in Andalucía and the Costa del Sol you simply shouldn't miss, and it's these attractions that make the Top 10. Discover what makes each one a must-see on the following pages.

CÓRDOBA
Aracena
Écija
HUELVA
Seville
Alcalá de Guadaira
Osuna
Olmera
Jerez de la Frontera
San Fernando
Estepona
Costa de la Luz

1. The Alhambra
2. Seville Cathedral and La Giralda
3. Real Alcázar, Seville
4. Córdoba
5. Cádiz
6. Ronda
7. The Costa del Sol
8. Baeza and Úbeda
9. Parque Nacional de Doñana
10. The Sierra Nevada

Guadalmez
Montoro
Linares
JAÉN
Jódar
Jaén
Guadajoz
Montilla
Alcaudete
Alcalá
la Real
Estepa
GRANADA
Antequera
MÁLAGA
Málaga
Nerja
Motril
Torremolinos
Marbella
Mediterranean Sea
0 kilometres 25
0 miles 25
4
8
8
1
10
7

1

THE ALHAMBRA

V3 C/Real de La Alhambra s/n, Granada Hours vary, check website Mon, 1 Jan & 25 Dec tickets.alhambra-patronato.es

With nearly two million visitors annually, the Alhambra is the most visited monument in Spain. This well-preserved medieval Arab palace stands atop Sabika Hill overlooking the city of Granada. During the Nasrid dynasty, it was transformed into a masterpiece of Islamic architecture and design. Note, visitors must show official ID for entry.

1 Puerta de la Justicia

Built in 1348, the "Justice Gate" horseshoe arch makes use of Arab defensive techniques – a steep approach combined with four right-angled turns – intended to slow down invading armies.

2 Puerta del Vino

One of the oldest structures in the complex, the "Wine Gate" – named for its use as a wine cellar in the 16th century – once served as the main entrance to the *medina* (market).

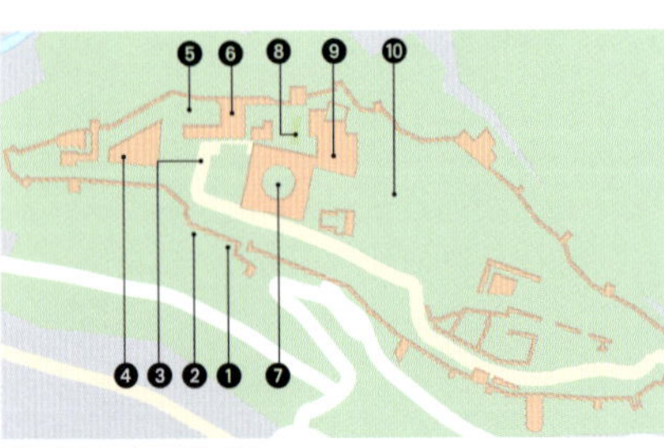

The Alhambra Site Plan

3 Plaza de los Aljibes

From these ramparts, visitors can enjoy superb views of Granada. The giant *aljibes* (cisterns) underneath were built by the Christian successors.

4 Alcazaba

Although largely in ruins, this fortress is well worth a visit. Don't miss climbing up onto the Torre de la Vela for views of the Sierra Nevada.

5 Palacios Nazaríes

Three stunning palaces, de Mexuar, de Comares and de los Leones, stand as the impressive

The remarkable Alhambra

Circular courtyard, Palacio de Carlos V

TOP TIP

There is limited entry, so be sure to book tickets online in advance.

centrepieces of the Alhambra. Built of simple brick, wood and stucco, so as not to compete with the creations of Allah.

6 Palacio de Mexuar

The most poorly preserved of the three palaces, the Palacio de Mexuar was the most public space, dedicated to judicial and bureaucratic business. Its original structure dates from 1365, but in the 16th century the Christians converted it to a chapel.

7 Palacio de Carlos V

This Italian Renaissance palace, a masterpiece by Michelangelo's student Pedro Machuca, houses two museums: the Museo de Bellas Artes and the Museo de la Alhambra *(958 02 79 29)*.

8 Palacio de Comares

Built in the mid-14th century, this area constituted the Serallo, where the sultan would receive dignitaries and deal with diplomatic issues. Inside is the Salón de Embajadores, the main throne room of the Alhambra. In front of the palace is the Patio de Arrayanes.

9 Palacio de los Leones

Dating from the late 1300s, this palace served as the Harem, the sultan's private living quarters. In its central courtyard, a fountain with 12 lions – Fuente de los Leones – is thought to symbolize the 12 signs of the zodiac, the 12 hours of the clock or the 12 tribes of Israel.

Fountain in the Palacio de los Leones

10 Jardínes del Partal

As you exit the Alhambra, stroll through the gardens, where watercourses wind through a landscape that once housed palaces. Today, only five porticoed arches remain, leading to the Generalife *(p24)*.

HISTORY OF THE ALHAMBRA

The Alhambra was the final stronghold of al-Andalus, the Muslim-ruled region of the Iberian Peninsula. By 1237, Christians had reconquered all but this emirate. The Moors held it for another 250 years until 1492, when Fernando II and Isabel I completed the Reconquista. Though later neglected and damaged – including an attempt by Napoleon to destroy it – restoration began in the 19th century, following the popularity of American writer Washington Irving's *Tales of the Alhambra* *(p59)*.

The Alhambra: Generalife

Intricate carved stucco, Torre de la Cautiva

1. The Name of the Garden

The word *Generalife* is generally considered to be a corruption of the Arab phrase *Djinat al-Arif*, which can be translated as "the Architect's Garden" (referring to Allah) or simply the "Best" or "High" garden. The Darro River was diverted 18 km (11 miles) to provide water for this lush sanctuary.

2. The Towers

Following the gardens of the Partal *(p23)* as you walk towards the Generalife, you will encounter a number of restored Moorish towers built into the wall. The Torre de los Picos, Torre del Cadí, Torre de la Cautiva, Torre de las Infantas, Torre del Cabo de la Carrera and Torre del Agua are all worth a visit for their fine detail, as well as for the views they command. The Torre de la Cautiva and the Torre de las Infantas are twin tower-palaces with richly decorated rooms.

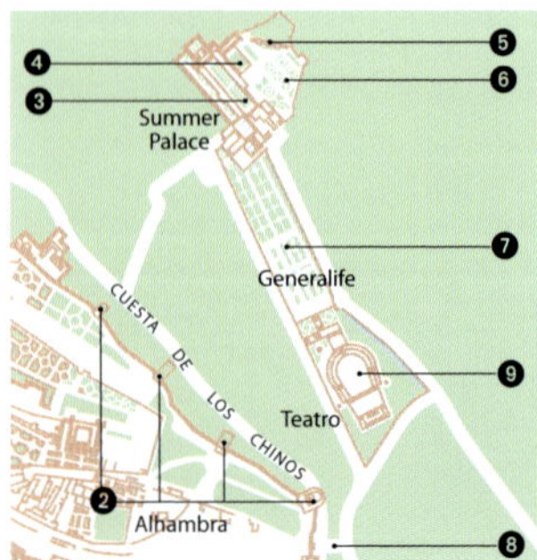

Generalife Site Plan

3. Patio de la Acequia

The "Courtyard of the Water Channel" is the most famous water spectacle of the garden. Perfectly proportioned pools are set off by rows of water jets. At one end stands one of the complex's most harmonious buildings, the Sala Regia, with its decorated arcades and airy portico. Previously, a small lookout existed here, though only its remains are visible today.

4. Patio de los Cipreses

An intimate court with a Baroque garden, the Courtyard of the Cypresses is also known as the Patio of the Sultana. It is believed to be the secret meeting place of Zoraya, wife of Boabdil, and her lover, the chief of the Abencerrajes clan. The sultan had the chief's men massacred upon discovery of the infidelity. A 700-year-old cypress tree commemorates the trysting place.

5. Escalera del Agua

Best viewed in spring, these staircases above the palace – also known as the *Camino de las Cascadas* – have handrails that double as watercourses.

6. Jardines Altos

At the entrance to the upper gardens is the Patio de Polo, where visitors would leave their horses before ascending to the palace. On this level there is a series of fountains and formal plantings, joined by walkways and copses. From here, you can also enjoy sweeping panoramic views.

7. Jardines Nuevos

The "New Gardens", also called the Lower Gardens, owe little to Moorish taste. Arched rose bushes, hedges and formal patterns echo Italian style, but the sound of running water creates an atmosphere in keeping with the Moorish ideal. In Islam, paradise is defined as an oasis – a water garden full of blossoms.

8. The Hill of the Sun

A footbridge flanked by two towers takes you over to the hill that rises above the Alhambra. A vast summer palace once stood here, amid an enormous garden, which predated the Alhambra by more than a century, although little of it remains today.

9. Teatro

While climbing the hill, you will find the amphitheatre, nestled into a tree-lined hollow. Dance performances and musical concerts are held here as part of an annual festival of the arts.

Relaxing in the beautiful, open-air Teatro

10. Leaving the Gardens

As you exit the gardens you will pass along the Paseo de las Adelfas and the Paseo de los Cipreses, lined respectively with oleanders and cypresses. Back to the Hill of the Sun, stroll down the pretty Cuesta del Rey Chico to the Albaicín *(p124)*.

er jets at the Patio de la Acequia

SEVILLE CATHEDRAL AND LA GIRALDA

M3 Plaza Virgen de los Reyes 11am–6pm daily (from 2:30pm Sun)
catedraldesevilla.es

Seville's cathedral, Europe's largest, is notable for its sheer size and its mighty Moorish bell tower, La Giralda. Built on the site of a 12th-century mosque erected by the Almohads, it became the main place of worship for Christian forces after their takeover in 1248. After the mosque was demolished in 1401, it took over a century to erect the new cathedral.

1 Exterior and Scale

In sheer cubic vastness, Seville Cathedral is the largest Christian church in the world, and there's a certificate from the Guinness Book of Records on display here to prove it. It measures 126 m (415 ft) by 83 m (270 ft) and the nave rises to 43 m (140 ft). The best place to take it all in is from its bell tower, La Giralda.

2 Puerta del Perdón

Set in a crenellated wall, the Puerta del Perdón or "Gate of Forgiveness" is the main entrance to the only surviving part of the mosque. A masterpiece of Almohad art, it features arches and bronze doors intricately carved with 880 Qur'anic inscriptions and bas-reliefs that show Renaissance influences.

> **VIEW**
> For great views and an immersive experience, time your climb up the Giralda tower to coincide with the ringing of its bells, which chime on the hour.

3 Patio de los Naranjos

Before entering the mosque for prayers, ritual ablutions were performed

Seville Cathedral complex and La Giralda

Paintings in the Sacristía Mayor

in this patio, also known as the Courtyard of Orange Trees.

4 Interior

The vast Gothic arches that line the nave inside the cathedral are so high that the space within the building is said to have its own climate.

5 Sala Capitular

The Chapter House has a lavish marble floor, and its vaulted ceiling is adorned with Murillo's *Immaculate Conception*.

6 La Giralda

Built between 1172 and 1195, this grand tower has become the symbol of Seville. It takes its name from *El Giraldillo*, the bronze female statue that adorns its top. Climb to the top for stunning city views.

Seville Cathedral Site Plan

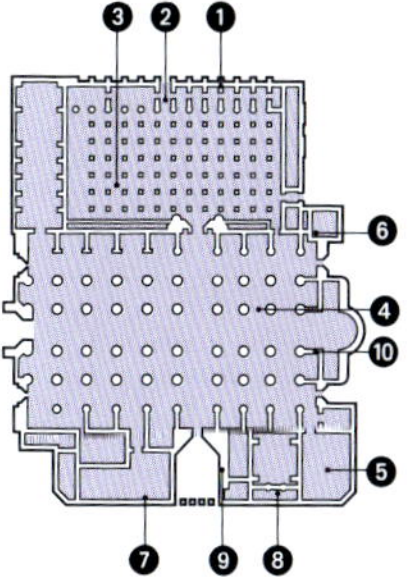

7 Sacristía Mayor

The main sacristy is notable for its impressive 16th-century dome. It's centrepiece is a 450-kg (990-lb), 3-m (10-ft) silver Baroque monstrance created by Spanish engraver Juan de Arfe.

8 Cathedral Paintings

There are around 600 paintings throughout the cathedral, from its entrance pavilion to the sacristies. These are accompanied by sculptures from the 17th-century Sevillian School, including artists such as Bartolomé Esteban Murillo, Francisco de Zurbarán and Francisco Pacheco.

9 Sacristía de los Cálices

Part of the cathedral's treasury is housed here. The anteroom displays the Tenebrario, a 7.8-m (25-ft) Plateresque candelabrum used during Holy Week. Inside, highlights include a painting by Goya of Seville's patron saints, Justa and Rufina, as well as canvases by Zurbarán, Jordaens and other masters.

SEMANA SANTA FESTIVITIES

Andalucía's most important Holy Week celebrations *(p84)* are held in Seville. During this time, 71 *cofradías* (brotherhoods) bear aloft the ornately dressed Virgin Mary in mourning as well as scenes from the Passion of Christ. These elaborate floats are carried by *costaleros* (bearers), while the processions are led by *nazarenos* (penitents) in hoods and robes.

10 Capilla Mayor

The Capilla Mayor, or main chapel, features a remarkable 15th-century *retablo* – the world's largest altarpiece. Made of gilded carved wood, it showcases 45 biblical scenes with some 1,000 figures.

Gothic interior of the Capilla Mayor

REAL ALCÁZAR, SEVILLE

M4 Patio de Banderas 9:30am–7pm daily (Oct–Mar: to 5pm) 1 & 6 Jan, Good Friday & 25 Dec alcazarsevilla.org

Home to Spanish kings for nearly seven centuries, the Real Alcázar is a masterpiece of Mudéjar architecture. Built atop Roman ruins in 913 CE by Emir Abd ar-Rahman III, it was expanded by caliphs and Christian kings like Pedro I. Set in a huge paradise garden, it showcases extravagant palatial rooms from multiple eras.

1 Puerta del León

Flanked by original Almohad walls, the Puerta del León leads into the first courtyard. A carved lion above the arch gives the gate its name, while its interior façade has a mix of Gothic and Arabic inscriptions.

2 Sala de Justicia

Here you'll find some of the finest Mudéjar art commissioned by Alfonso XI of Castile around 1330 and executed by crafters from Granada. The star-shaped coffered ceiling and intricate plasterwork are particularly noteworthy.

TOP TIP

A flow-control entry system allows limited visitors, so try to visit during off-peak times.

3 Patio del Yeso

The Patio del Yeso, or Courtyard of Plaster, is one of the few remnants of the 12th-century palace. Its delicate stuccowork, featuring scalloped arches, is surrounded by a garden with water channels, paying homage to water. Together with the Sala de Justicia, this courtyard is among the oldest parts of the site.

4 Patio de las Doncellas

Probably the best-known part of the palace, the Courtyard of the Maidens commemorates the annual tribute of 100 virgins once offered by the Christians to the Moorish rulers. Look out for the fine *azulejos* (tiles).

Central pool, Patio de las Doncellas

Clockwise from above **Landscaped gardens in the complex; *azulejos* and plaster-work, Salón de los Embajadores; stuccowork on a wall; Puerta del León or Lion Gate**

5 Salón de Embajadores

This is the most stunning room in the complex, featuring a wooden dome, carved, painted and gilded, by artisans from Toledo and completed in 1366.

6 Patio de las Muñecas

A private living space, the Courtyard of the Dolls supposedly gets its name from two faces carved into the base of one of its arches.

Real Alcázar Site Plan

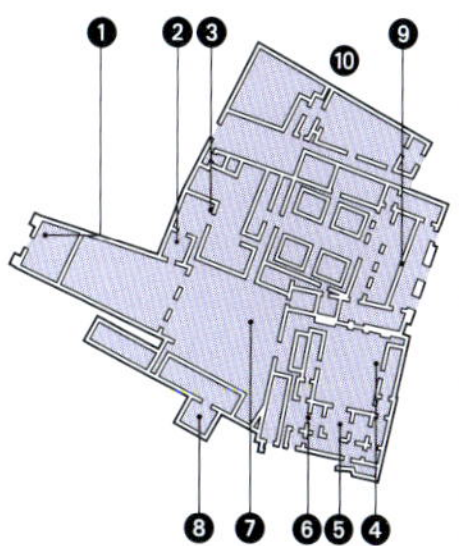

7 Patio de la Montería

The Hunting Courtyard gets its name from the royal hunters who gathered here before their expeditions. It's a perfect mix of cultural influences, featuring 14th-century Mudéjar decorative work.

8 Casa de la Contratación

At the Casa de la Contratación, or House of Trade, Spanish monarchs Fernando and Isabel met with the explorers of the Americas to manage trade flows.

9 Palacio Gótico

Set in a refurbished 13th-century Gothic structure built by Alfonso X the Wise, this palace has a rather inharmonious Renaissance style.

10 Gardens

The palace gardens are rich in Moorish influences, featuring many fountains, pools, orange groves, palms and hedgerows. In the summer, the gardens host concerts and other events in the lighter evenings.

PEDRO I

Few Spanish kings have received such contradictory press over the centuries as Pedro I (r.1350–69). Called both "the Cruel" – el Cruel – and "the Avenger" – el Justiciero – he killed his own brother in order to consolidate his position and flaunted his cohabitation with his mistress, María de Padilla. The Alcázar we see today is almost entirely the result of Pedro's rebuilding programme, primarily so that he and María would have a cosy place of retreat.

CÓRDOBA

D3

A jewel in Andalucía's crown, Córdoba is home to the Great Mosque, La Mezquita, an unsurpassed architectural gem. Alongside the mosque and its incongruous but splendid cathedral, the city offers an array of remarkable sights including fine monuments and palaces from every era, excellent art and history museums, one of Andalucía's greatest archaeological repositories, and a museum dedicated to the history of bullfighting.

1 Judería

1.5 km (1 mile) from the city centre

Dating back to the Roman Empire, the city's ancient Jewish quarter features narrow alleyways and beautiful Moorish patios. This district also houses Andalucía's only medieval synagogue *(p49)*.

2 Museo Taurino

Plaza de Maimónides Mon museotaurinodecordoba.es

Dedicated to bullfighting, this museum has a fine collection of related art. Its exhibits trace the history of the tradition and rearing of the bulls, and highlights key bullfighting figures.

3 Baños del Alcázar Califal

Campo Santo de los Mártires 957 42 01 51 Mon

Once part of the caliph's palace, this well-preserved 10th-century Moorish bathhouse showcases its impressive underfloor heating system.

Colourful buildings lining a street, Judería

4 Alcázar de los Reyes Cristianos

Adjacent to the Baños del Alcázar Califal is the Alcázar de los Reyes Cristianos *(p65)*. Built in 1328, this fortified palace was used by the Inquisition (1500s–1820) and later served as a prison (until the 1950s). Today, it is known for its tranquil gardens, water terraces and fountains.

Córdoba's grand La Mezquita

5 Puente Romano

Crossing the Río Guadalquivir, this Roman bridge is adorned with a statue of the Archangel Raphael, who is said to have saved the city from the plague.

6 Museo Torre de la Calahorra

Puente Romano
Hours vary, check website
torrecalahorra.es

Part of a Moorish castle that controlled access to the city, this tower now houses the Roger Garaudy Three Cultures Museum, which explains how all religions lived side by side in medieval Córdoba and displays exhibits from the time. The tower also offers excellent city views.

7 Museo de Bellas Artes

Plaza del Potro 1
957 10 36 59
Summer: 9am–3pm Tue–Sun; winter: 9am–9pm Tue–Sat (to 3pm Sun)

A former 16th-century charity hospital, this building is now the city's main art museum. It has works by local painters and sculptors, as well as paintings and drawings by masters such as Goya, Ribera, Murillo, Valdés Leal and Zurbarán.

8 Museo Arqueológico

Housed in a Renaissance mansion, this excellent archaeological museum *(p57)* displays a 10th-century Moorish bronze of a stag, which was found at Medina Azahara *(p131)*.

9 Palacio de los Marqueses de Viana

Plaza Don Gome 2
Hours vary, check website
palaciodeviana.com

A former noble residence dating from the 14th to the 18th centuries, this palace features 12 courtyards and a garden, showcasing a blend of Roman and Arabic styles. It now houses a museum with preserved period rooms and furnishings.

MULTICULTURAL TRADITION

Córdoba owes much to its rich multicultural history. Its most important edifices are emblematic of the amalgamation of Islamic, Christian and Jewish cultures. In the 10th century, the city was the spiritual and scientific centre of the Western World, due to its policy of religious tolerance. After the Reconquista, many non-Christian thinkers were banished and thereafter the city fell into decline.

10 La Mezquita

The world's third-largest mosque, La Mezquita *(p32)* remains a place of immense grandeur and mystical power.

Patio in the Palacio de los Marqueses de Viana

Córdoba: La Mezquita

1. Choir Stalls

Dating from 1758, the Baroque choir stalls are created from exquisitely carved mahogany and depict various biblical scenes. Their crowning glory is a figure of the Archangel Raphael.

2. Puerta del Perdón

Originally the mosque had many entrances, designed to let in light. Today, however, only the Gate of Forgiveness (1377) remains open to the public. Above its arch, there are images of St Stephen, the Assumption of the Virgin and St Michael.

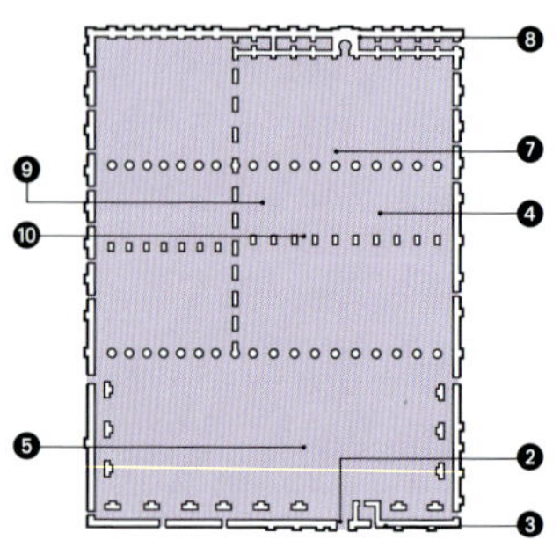

La Mezquita Site Plan

3. Torre del Alminar

An iconic symbol of the city, this Baroque bell tower is the highest point in Córdoba. It occupies the same spot where a minaret, built in 957, once stood.

4. Interior

La Mezquita's interior, described as a "forest" mosque, features 856 variegated columns and rows of arches designed to resemble palm trees. Unlike Christian churches, which are usually inspired by Roman basilicas and focus on a central enthroned "divine judge", Islamic mosques aim to induce a meditative state for prayer.

5. Patio de los Naranjos

Once a site for ritual ablutions before prayer, the Courtyard of the Orange Trees has been transformed into a beautiful garden. Today, it is home to orange trees and palms that have been planted to mirror the columns inside the prayer hall.

6. Recycled Columns

Great ingenuity was required to achieve the rhythmic uniformity inside, since most of the columns used in

Horseshoe arches in the mihrab

construction were recycled from Roman, Visigothic and other sources. They were a hotchpotch of varying sizes, so the longer ones had to be sunk into the floor. To reach the desired height, a second tier was then added.

7. Capilla de Villaviciosa and Capilla Real

One of the more grand Christian additions, the Villaviciosa Chapel, built in 1377, has exuberant Mudéjar arches. Next to it, the Royal Chapel has stuccowork and *azulejos* (tiles).

8. Mihrab

Dating from the 10th century, this octagonal chamber, set into the wall, is the jewel of the mosque. It was designed to be the sacred focal point of prayers directed towards Mecca. No expense was spared in its ornamentation, with Emperor Nicephorus III sending artisans from Constantinople to create some of the finest Byzantine mosaics.

9. Cathedral

In 1523, around 400 of the original 1200 columns were removed from the mosque to make way for the cathedral, and a high altar and chapels were built along the quadrangle.

10. The Caliphal Style

Begun by Caliph Abd el-Rahman I in 786 CE, La Mezquita marks the beginning of the Caliphal architectural style, blending Roman, Gothic, Byzantine, Syrian and Persian elements.

Red-and-white striped Caliphal arches

CÁDIZ

B5

The coastal city of Cádiz, once admired by poets like Lord Byron for its striking seaside views, is today a vibrant hub known for its festive spirit. According to ancient chronicles, Cádiz was founded by the Phoenicians as Gadir ("Fortress") in 1104 BCE, giving it a claim to being Europe's oldest city. Later, under the Romans it became Gades and was the city where Julius Caesar held his first public office.

1 Oratorio de la Santa Cueva

C/Rosario 10

This Neo-Classical chapel has an upper church adorned with Ionic columns and three exquisite frescoes by Goya.

2 Hospital de Mujeres

C/Hospital de Mujeres 26 10:30am–4pm Mon–Fri

The *Extasis de San Francisco* by El Greco is the main attraction at this former Baroque hospital.

SHOP

Popular store Sasha Alpargatas *(p113)* offers a stylish and comfortable range of espadrilles for men and women, crafted from a range of natural materials.

3 Torre Tavira

C/Marqués del Real Tesoro 10 956 21 29 10 10am–6pm daily (May–Sep: to 8pm)

Perched atop the city's highest tower at 46 m (150 ft), the *camera obscura* offers stunning views of the city. Guided tours are available in English, Spanish and French.

4 Plaza de las Flores

Also known as the Plaza de Topete, this square was once home to a Phoenician temple.

5 Barrio del Pópulo

The medieval heart of the city, the Barrio del Pópulo is home to

Clockwise from below **Terracotta busts on display in the Museo de Cádiz; historical arch, Barrio del Pópulo; steps leading to the ruins of Cádiz's Roman theatre**

Palm trees lining the Plaza San Juan de Dios

three 13th-century gates. Nearby, the Puerta de Tierra, the main entrance in the surviving 18th-century city wall, marks the boundary between the old city and the modern part of Cádiz.

6 Iglesia de Santa Cruz

⌂ Plaza Fray Félix 6

In the midst of the Barrio del Pópulo are the ruins of a Roman theatre and a church dating from 1260. Artifacts excavated from the site are displayed in an on-site museum.

7 Plaza San Juan de Dios

This 16th-century plaza *(p64)*, located on the edge of the Barrio del Pópulo and facing the port, serves as the central hub of city life.

8 Catedral Nueva

⌂ Plaza Pío XII s/n
☎ 956 28 61 54 ◷ Hours vary, call ahead

Construction of the "New Cathedral" began in 1722. Its bell tower, or Torre de Poniente (western tower), offers impressive views.

9 Museo de Cádiz

The Museo de Cádiz *(p57)* displays archaeological finds and Baroque paintings, including Roman shipwreck finds and a pair of 5th-century BCE Phoenician sarcophagi.

10 Museo de las Cortes de Cádiz

⌂ C/Sta. Inés 9

This popular museum is known for its mural, which eulogizes Cádiz as the birthplace of liberalism. On 29 March 1812, Spain's first liberal constitution was drawn up in Cadiz – an event that played a significant role in shaping early modern European politics *(p49)*.

LOS CARNAVALES

The vibrant Carnaval *(p84)* celebrations in this port city are the most exhilarating in all of Spain. Here was the only event that Franco's forces failed to suppress during his dictatorship. The festival's various traditions date back to the 15th century, when the city had a Genoese enclave, though some claim there is also a strong Cuban influence. It is advisable to book your hotel up to a year in advance, as the celebrations attract huge crowds.

RONDA

D5

Ronda, the most famous of the region's *pueblos blancos*, sits in the Serranía de Ronda, a mountainous region between Málaga, Algeciras and Seville. Just a half-hour drive from the Costa del Sol, it retains its timeless charm. Perched above a plunging gorge and connected by a dramatic 18th-century bridge, its setting is truly striking.

1 Casa del Rey Moro

C/Cuesta de Santo Domingo 9 Hours vary, check website casadelreymoro.org

Built on the foundations of a Moorish palace, this 18th-century mansion features lovely gardens with superb views.

2 Palacio del Marqués de Salvatierra

C/Real 2

The carved stone portal outside this 18th-century mansion features four imposing figures that are believed to represent the Indigenous Peoples of South America.

3 Palacio de Mondragón

Plaza Mondragón s/n 952 87 08 18 Hours vary, call ahead

Dating back to 1314, this is one of Ronda's most beautiful palaces, with original mosaics and a Mudéjar ceiling. A section now serves as Ronda's archaeological museum.

4 Puente Nuevo

1.5 km (1 mile) from the centre

Ronda perches upon a sheer outcrop that is split by a precipitous cleft, El Tajo, 100 m (330 ft) deep (right). The spectacular 18th-century Puente Nuevo bridge links the old city, La Ciudad, with the new.

5 Puente Viejo

1 km (half a mile) from the centre

The Puente Viejo (Old Bridge), dating from 1616 and sometimes mistakenly referred to as the "Roman" bridge, is actually of Moorish origin, like the nearby Puente de San Miguel.

6 Minarete de San Sebastián

Plaza Abul Beka s/n

This 14th-century tower is all that remains of a Nasrid mosque and the church of San Sebastián that was built on top of it.

Dramatic cliffside setting of Ronda

Admiring the walls of Baños Árabes

7 Baños Árabes

These well-preserved Moorish baths *(p53)* date from the 1200s or early 1300s. It features the typical multiple barrel vaulting, pierced with star-shaped lunettes.

8 Museo Lara Coleccionismo

C/Armiñán 29 Hours vary, check website museolara.org

With over 2,000 works, this museum holds the largest private collection in Spain. Objects include cultural artifacts, antique clocks, weapons and scientific instruments.

9 Plaza de Toros

C/Virgen de la Paz 15 Hours vary, check website rmcr.org

Inaugurated in 1785, Ronda's bullring is the widest in the world and one of the oldest in Spain. It also houses the Museo Taurino, a museum dedicated to the tradition.

10 Iglesia de Santa María la Mayor

Plaza Duquesa de Parcent 952 87 40 48 10am–8pm Mon–Sat, 10am–12:30pm & 2–8pm Sun

This church was built into the structure of a 13th century mosque. The square-shaped belfry is a visible reminder of the church's Islamic past.

THE ORIGINS OF BULLFIGHTING

The creation of the *Real Maestranza de Caballería* (Royal Academy of Knights) in 1572 set the stage for the birth of bullfighting, as the aristocrats on horseback challenged wild bulls. In the 18th century, Francisco Romero pioneered the practice of fighting bulls on foot. His grandson, Pedro (1749–1839), later perfected the art. Bullfighting is entwined with southern Spanish culture, but remains controversial due to its violent nature. If attending a corrida, seek an experienced matador for a "cleaner" kill *(p145)*.

7

THE COSTA DEL SOL

D5–E5

Once home to quiet fishing villages, the "Sun Coast" now draws millions of visitors annually, not counting the estimated 300,000 expats residing here. With 320 sunny days a year, it offers plenty to enjoy. While neon and tower blocks dominate, the true Andalucían spirit shines through in the lively atmosphere, where visitors soak up the sun and enjoy the vibrant pace of life.

1 Estepona

D5

Estepona was among the first major resorts on this coast, with 19 km (12 miles) of beach. Its *casco antiguo* (old town) is home to the charming Plaza Las Flores.

2 Marbella

Spain's most expensive resort, Marbella *(p69)* features the 15th-century Plaza de los Naranjos in the heart of its old town. Nearby Puerto Banús is the town's glittering marina, where you can admire the fabulous yachts and luxurious lifestyles.

Yachts docked at the port, Marbella

EAT

Espetos – grilled sardines – are a traditional local speciality in the Málaga province. Try this salty, smoky dish at El Canarias *(p115)*.

3 Fuengirola

D5

This resort town is perfect for families, featuring a beautiful beach and a scenic seafront promenade. Nearby, there's also a restored 10th-century Moorish castle.

Estepona's lovely old town

VIEW
El Balcón de Europa, located in the town of Nerja, has amazing views of the surrounding mountains and miles of sea.

4 Benalmádena
D5

This resort offers three distinct areas for enjoyment: the old town inland, a beach and port area and the Arroyo de la Miel, a lively suburb.

5 Mijas
D5

A charming mountain village, Mijas features a maze of old Moorish streets, filled with shops and restaurants. From here, there are great views of the coast.

6 Torremolinos

Torre de los Molinos (Tower of the Windmills) refers to a Moorish watchtower, once surrounded by 19 flourmills. Today the town is a hub for the region's largest LGBTQ+ community *(p69)*.

7 Málaga

Andalucía's second-largest city, Málaga *(p108)* has outposts of Paris's Pompidou Centre and the State Russian Museum. The redeveloped port is home to dozens of dining options while the nearby Soho district brings art to the streets.

8 Torre del Mar

To the west, this resort *(p69)* is popular among holidaymakers and a family favourite.

9 Vélez-Málaga
E5

This market town has beautiful Mudéjar features and a lively annual flamenco guitar competition every July.

10 Nerja

This coastal town *(p69)* sits on verdant cliffs, with quiet pebble beach coves below. Nearby, the Cuevas de Nerja *(p76)* offer an impressive network of remarkable prehistoric caves.

View from El Balcón de Europa, Nerja

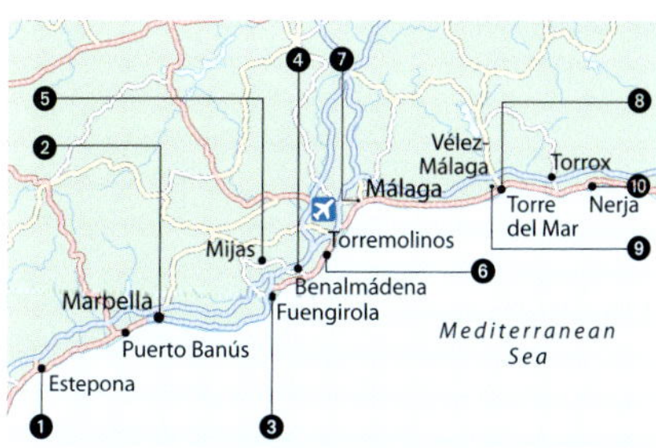

BAEZA AND ÚBEDA

F2 Baeza: turismo.baeza.net; Úbeda: turismodeubeda.com

These two Jaén Province cities, 9 km (5.5 miles) apart, are like matching jewel boxes of Renaissance architectural treasure, and were declared UNESCO World Heritage Sites in 2003. While Baeza has largely stayed untouched by the modern age, Úbeda is now a thriving city with many attractions, though its historic district remains its highlight.

1 Plaza del Pópulo, Baeza

The Plaza del Pópulo, also known as the Square of the Lions, is Baeza's most charming area. This elegant Renaissance square is home to a fountain featuring four stone lions, carved in the village of Cástulo, and a female statue believed to represent Imilce, a princess who married the Carthaginian general Hannibal.

DRINK

Enjoy a drink in the heart of the town hall square at Mesón Navarro *(p135)*, where you can enjoy great views from the terrace.

2 Puerta de Jaén, Baeza

This Jaén Gate was once part of Baeza's ancient wall. It supports an arch bearing a coat of arms.

3 Plaza Santa María, Baeza

Several glorious 16th-century structures, including a cathedral, front this square. One of the many masterpieces by Renaissance architect Andrés de Vandelvira, the cathedral was originally a Gothic church, built over a mosque in the 13th century. In the centre, a large fountain honours the arrival of water in Baeza.

***Fuente de Los Leones*, Plaza del Pópulo, Baeza**

4 Paseo de la Constitución, Baeza

This promenade *(p65)* is a popular meeting spot and houses the 16th-century Alhóndiga (corn exchange) with its elegant arches. The Torre de los Aliatares, a remnant of the old wall, is also located here.

5 Plaza del Primero de Mayo, Úbeda

This plaza has many attractions. These include the Iglesia de San Pablo, with an array of styles, the 15th-century Casa Mudéjar – now an archaeology museum – and the 16th-century Ayuntamiento Viejo, with superb arcades.

ARCHITECTURE OF THE SPANISH RENAISSANCE

Spanish Renaissance architecture is divided into three periods: Plateresque, Classical High Renaissance and Herrerean. The first refers to the carved detailing on silverwork (*platero* means silversmith), a carry-over from the late Gothic style popular under Queen Isabel. The Classical High Renaissance style is noted for its symmetry and its Greco Roman imagery. Herrerean works are very sober, practically devoid of decoration.

6 Plaza San Lorenzo, Úbeda

While the Church of San Lorenzo is the highlight of this square, the towers and gargoyles of the Casa de las Torres are equally impressive.

7 Plaza de San Pedro, Úbeda

Visit the patio of the Real Monasterio de Santa Clara, the town's oldest church, where the nuns will sell you their distinctly Arabic *dulces* (sweetcakes). Nearby, the Palacio de la Rambla is another Vandelvira creation, now a luxury hotel.

8 The Pottery Quarter, Úbeda

The Puerta del Losal, a splendid 13th-century Mudéjar gate, takes you into the town's age-old pottery quarter *(p134)*. Here, along Calle Valencia, modern ceramic artists renowned all over Spain and beyond practise their ancient trade. Among these, the Tito family are famous as the leading ceramists in Úbeda.

Entrance to the Palacio de Jabalquinto, Baeza

9 Palacio de Jabalquinto, Baeza

Considered one of the most unusually decorated palaces, the 15th-century Palacio de Jabalquinto *(p51)* is sprinkled with coats of arms and stone studs in Isabelline Plateresque style.

10 Plaza de Vázquez de Molina, Úbeda

The Capilla del Salvador, a highlight of the Spanish Renaissance, is notable for its Plateresque front on this square.

Vases in the Pottery Quarter, Úbeda

9

PARQUE NACIONAL DE DOÑANA

B4 Huelva & Sevilla Hours vary, check website
donanareservas.com

Established in 1969, the Parque Nacional de Doñana is an important wetland reserve and a prime site for migrating birds. It covers more than 2,470 sq km (954 sq miles) and is designated as a UNESCO Biosphere Reserve due to its wide variety of ecosystems, rare fauna and abundance of birdlife.

1 Setting and History

Located at the estuary of the Guadalquivir River, the area probably owes its present pristine condition to the fact that it was set aside as a hunting preserve for the nobility in the 16th century.

2 Visitor Centres

The park's visitor centres host various exhibitions as well as planned trails, with rest areas and bird-watching options.

3 Guided Tours

All-terrain vehicles depart from the visitor centres twice daily, with itineraries dependent on the time of year. The marshes dry up during the summer months, limiting bird-watching, but this increases the chance of seeing rare wildlife.

Strolling a boardwalk in the park

4 Habitats

The park features three distinct kinds of ecosystem: dunes, *coto*

Greater flamingos fishing on a marsh

ECOLOGICAL ISSUES

In 1998, a Río Tinto toxic waste reservoir burst, dumping pollutants into the Río Guadiamar, one of the wetlands' main tributaries. Thankfully, the wave of acids was stopped just short of the park, but damage was done to its border areas. Today, the region is under threat due to lack of rainfall and illegal water irrigation.

TOP TIP

Carry binoculars, mosquito repellent, and sunscreen, and watch out for quicksand.

(pine and cork forests and scrubland) and *marisma* (wetlands), which in turn comprise marshes, salt marshes, lagoons and floodplains.

5 El Palacio de Acebrón

Carretera A-483, El Rocío

This Neo-Classical-style hunting lodge, built in 1961, hosts an exhibition on the history and ethnography of the region. It is also the starting point for a 12-km (8-mile) woodland trail.

6 Huts

Dating from the 18th century, these traditional, uninhabited huts are found in the *pinares* (pine forests). They are constructed with pine frames covered in local thatch.

7 Bird Shelter

The main visitor centre, the Centro de Visitantes El Acebuche, is set on a lagoon. At its eastern end, there is an aviary where birds receive intensive care.

8 El Rocío's Romería

This town is the focal point of one of Spain's largest festivals, the Romería del Rocío *(p84)*. This four-day pilgrimage leading up to Whitsun winds its way through the park to honour the Virgin of El Rocío.

9 Flora

Umbrella pines and cork oaks flourish here and both provide crucial nesting sites for birds. Wild flowers in the dunes and scrubland areas include the pink spiny-leafed thrift, besom heath, yellow gorse and the bubil lily.

10 Fauna

The endangered Iberian lynx is the emblem of the park. This area is home to at least 300,000 birds, including flamingos and purple gallinules. Around 25 pairs of the rare Iberian eagle also reside here.

Iberian lynx resting on a cliff

10

THE SIERRA NEVADA

F4 Parque Nacional de la Sierra Nevada

Spain's highest mountain range and Europe's second-highest, the Sierra Nevada was once a main source of ice for Granada. Today, it's a popular destination for trekking, skiing and exploring the villages of Las Alpujarras. In 1999, the area was designated a national park, recognizing its natural beauty and cultural importance.

1 Setting

Mainland Spain's highest peak, the Mulhacén (3,482 m/11,425 ft), is at the western end of the mountain range.

2 Flora and Fauna

Snowcapped for most of the year, the mountains are still a haven for wild flowers. Some 140 unique varieties thrive here, including giant honeysuckle, various oak species and Granada sagebrush. The diverse fauna here includes the ibex and golden eagle.

3 Puerto del Suspiro del Moro

Heading south from Granada on the N323, you'll come to the spot known as the "Pass of the Moor's Sigh". Here, the bereft Boabdil (the last Moorish ruler in Spain), expelled by the Christians, is said to have looked back on his beloved city for the last time.

VIEW
Enjoy serene Sierra Nevada views from the Torre de la Vela in the Alhambra *(p22)*, one of the iconic towers of the famous palace.

4 Barranco de Poqueira

F4

This vast and gorgeous ravine is home to a stunning collection of tiny villages, offering breathtaking mountain views. For visitors seeking tranquillity, the remote site even has a Tibetan monastery, founded in 1982. The ravine is an excellent spot for easy day walks, and each village offers traditional local crafts.

Enjoying a chairlift ride in winter

EAT

Lovers of *jamón serrano* (mountain-cured ham) must try the snow-cured variety from any of the restaurants in the scenic town of Trevélez.

5 Las Alpujarras

The dramatic southern Sierra Nevada is home to this stunning series of white villages *(p53)*. The Moorish-style architecture found here, nearly identical to that of Morocco's Rif Mountains, features flat-roofed houses linked by small bridges.

6 Órgiva

F4

Made the regional capital in 1839, this town is at its best on Thursday mornings, when it comes alive for market day.

7 Lanjarón

F4

Famous since Roman times for its springs, this town is now a *balneario* (spa) and marks the beginning of the Alpujarras proper. Below the main street is a Moorish castle offering lovely views over the gorge.

8 Valle de Lecrín

F4

This bucolic valley is filled with almond, olive and citrus groves – the almond blossom is stunning in late winter.

9 Skiing

The Sierra Nevada is the best ski resort in Spain, with around 88 days of sunshine per season. April is the month with most snow, with an average depth of 237 cm (93 in) at the peak and 84 cm (33 in) at the base.

10 Hiking

There is a paved road over the top of the range but the uppermost reaches have been closed to cars since January 1999. In summer it becomes a hiker's paradise – the second-highest peak, Veleta (3,470 m/11,385 ft), is a relatively easy five-hour round trip.

BRENAN'S SOUTH FROM GRANADA

In the 1920s, British writer Gerald Brenan, a member of the Bloomsbury set, came to live in the village of Yegen in the eastern Alpujarras. He noted his experiences in his book *South from Granada*, a wonderful evocation of the place and its people, whose way of life is still largely unchanged. The 2002 Spanish film *Al Sur de Granada* is a delightful dramatization based on the book.

Clockwise from right **Native snapdragons in bloom; hiking a trail in the Sierra Nevada; stalls at a market selling traditional craft items**

TOP 10 OF EVERYTHING

A display of traditional flamenco fans

PLACES OF WORSHIP

1 Mosque, Almonaster la Real

B3 C/ 10, 21350 Almonaster la Real, Huelva 959 14 30 03
9am–8:30pm daily

Remarkably well-preserved for 1,000 years, this is one of Andalucía's few surviving rural mosques. It has Spain's oldest mihrab (Mecca-facing niche).

2 Iglesia de San Mateo, Lucena

E3 Plaza Nueva 7:30am–1:30pm & 7–9pm daily

It's intriguing to find one of the masterpieces of Andalucían Rococo design in this industrial town – Lucena was famous for having been a virtually independent Jewish enclave during Moorish rule. The 18th-century octagonal sacristy and decorative dome are the gems of this 15th-century church.

Main altar at Iglesia de San Mateo, Lucena

3 La Colegiata de la Asunción, Osuna

D4 Plaza la Encarnación 4
Hours vary, check website
colegiatadeosuna.es

Set on a hilltop, this massive Spanish Renaissance church dominates the town. Its austere façade is relieved by a fine Plateresque portal, the Puerta del Sol. The many treasures inside include five masterpieces by José de Ribera, a Crucifixion sculpture by Juan de Mesa, beautiful Renaissance ornamentation and a wonderful Baroque altarpiece.

4 Monasterio de San Jerónimo, Granada

F4 C/Rector López Argueta 9
958 27 93 37 Mar–Aug: 10am–1:30pm & 4–7:30pm daily; Sep–Feb: 10am–1pm & 3–6:30pm Mon–Sat

This Renaissance magnum opus is largely the creation of the great master, Diego de Siloé. The façade's upper window is flanked by sinuous mythological animals and medallions. The altar is monumental, consisting of row upon row of high reliefs framed by columns.

The red-and-white arches of La Mezquita

5 La Mezquita, Córdoba

This spectacular mosque *(p32)* may have been savagely reconsecrated but visitors can still see its Byzantine mosaics and other exquisite marvels.

6 Oratorio de San Felipe Neri, Cádiz

B5 Plaza San Felipe Neri 662 64 22 33 10:30am–4pm Mon–Fri, 9am–2pm Sat, 10am–noon Sun

As the commemorative plaques adorning the façade reveal, this fine Baroque church is one of the most significant buildings in Spain. On 29 March 1812, Spanish patriots defied a Napoleonic blockade and met here to compose the country's first constitution.

7 Sinagoga del Agua, Jaén

F2 C/Roque Rojas 2 953 75 81 50 Hours vary, call ahead

The Synagogue of Water was discovered during a construction project led by local entrepreneur Fernando Crespo. Dating back to before the 14th century, it features beautifully preserved arches, a women's gallery, an Inquisitor's room and a mikveh (ritual bath). The site is known for its traditional synagogue architecture and a courtyard with engraved columns. A cellar and ovens once used for kosher food preparation also highlight the presence of Úbeda's historic Jewish community.

8 Seville Cathedral

This vast cathedral *(p26)* is Seville's most striking architectural masterpiece. It has soaring columns, precious artworks and the world's largest altarpiece.

9 Sinagoga, Córdoba

D3 C/Judíos 20, Centro 957 01 53 34 Hours vary, call ahead

Built in the 14th century, the Córdoba Synagogue is one of Spain's best-preserved medieval synagogues. It showcases Mudéjar design, with a small courtyard, a prayer hall and a women's gallery. Actively used until the expulsion of the Jews in 1492, the synagogue served as a hospital and a chapel before being restored and reopened as a museum in 1985.

10 Catedral, Granada

Commissioned by the Catholic Monarchs, construction of this cathedral *(p120)* began in 1523 under architect Enrique de Egas. The work continued for over 180 years, with Diego de Siloé taking over in 1529. Inside is the stunning Capilla Real (Royal Chapel). At the chapel's sarcophagi, Isabel I's head presses more deeply into her marble pillow than that of Fernando II – said to indicate greater intelligence. In the Sacristy Museum, there are paintings by several 15th-century artists including Juan de Flandes and Sandro Botticelli.

Triumphal arch and the grand façade of Granada's cathedral

ALCÁZARES, PALACIOS AND CASTILLOS

Arches and mosaic flooring, La Casa de Pilatos, Seville

1 La Casa de Pilatos, Seville

Few palaces are more opulent than this 16th-century mansion *(p89)*. Featuring a mix of Mudéjar (Christian-Islamic), flamboyant Gothic and Renaissance styles, it is also adorned with Classical sculptures, including a 5th-century BCE Greek Athena and Roman works. A noble residence to this day, the mansion is filled with family portraits and antiques.

2 Real Alcázar, Seville

This resplendent palace *(p28)* and extensive gardens constitute a world of royal luxury. The architectural styles are a blend of mainly Moorish traditions – note the lavish use of the horseshoe arch, glazed tilework and wooden ceilings.

3 Fortaleza de la Mota, Alcalá la Real

E3 Castillo-Fortaleza de la Mota, 23680 10am–7pm daily (mid-Sep–Apr: to 6pm) fortalezadelamota.com

This Moorish castle crowns the hill above the town. Created by Granada's rulers in the 8th century, it incorporates 12th-century structures and earlier elements. After the Christian reconquest in 1341, additions to the fortress continued until the 16th century. The keep houses a visitor centre.

4 Palacio del Marqués de la Gomera, Osuna

D4 C/San Pedro 20 hotelpalaciodelmarques.es

Now a hotel and restaurant, this 18th-century palace is a striking example of the Spanish Baroque style. The family escutcheon crowns the carved stone doorway. Inside, the palace features a chapel with a gilded wooden altarpiece.

Elegant dining room in the Palacio de las Dueñas, Seville

5 Palacio de las Dueñas, Seville

M1 C/Dueñas 5 10am–6pm daily (summer: to 7pm) lasduenas.es

Built between the 15th and 16th centuries, this luxurious palace is the official city residence of the Duke of Alba. In addition to its magnificent architecture, Las Dueñas is also home to a vast collection of art and a beautiful garden.

6 Palacio de Jabalquinto, Baeza

F2 Plaza de Santa Cruz Hours vary, call ahead 953 77 99 82

The façade of this 15th-century palace defies categorization; the gallery and the patio evoke the Renaissance style.

7 Castillo de Santa Catalina, Jaén

F3 Carretera al Castillo Mid-Jun–mid-Sep: 10am–2pm & 5–9pm daily (to 3pm only Sun); mid-Sep–mid-Jun: 10am–6pm daily (to 3pm Sun) castillosantacatalina.es

Restored by the Christians, this 13th-century castle towers above the city and affords spectacular views, especially at sunset. Note, entry is free on Wednesday from 5pm to 9pm.

8 Castillo de Burgalimar, Baños de la Encina

F2 Cerro del Cueto, Plaza de Santa María 1 953 61 33 38 Hours vary, call ahead

This Moorish castle is one of the best preserved in Andalucía. Its horseshoe-arched main gate bears an inscription dating its construction to 967 CE. Some 14 square towers provide vistas far and wide.

9 Castillo de La Calahorra

F4 C/San Sebastián 958 67 70 98 10am–4:30pm Wed

One of the few castles built after the Christian reconquest, this was also one of the first in Spain to be built in Italian Renaissance style. Despite its intimidating setting and exterior, the inner courtyard is exquisite.

10 Castillo de Vélez Blanco

H3 C/Castillo s/n 607 41 50 55 Apr–Sep: 10am–2pm & 5–8pm Wed–Sun; Oct–Mar: 10am–2pm & 4–6pm Wed–Sun

This fairy-tale castle was unfortunately gutted in the early 1900s, but a reconstruction of one of the patios gives you some idea of its original splendour.

ASPECTS OF MOORISH HERITAGE

1 Religious Tolerance

Although non-Muslims had to pay a special tax and wear distinctive clothing, Moorish policies towards Jews and Catholics were generally easy-going. There was greater repression after the Almohads came into power in the 12th century, but mostly, various faiths were well integrated for many centuries.

2 Music

The Moors can be credited with the early development of the guitar *(p54)*, which they adapted from the four-stringed lute. The Middle Eastern musical forms they brought with them would later influence the development of flamenco.

3 Gardens

Moorish gardens make prominent use of water, which is especially important in a perpetually arid land. It was sprayed, channelled, made to gurgle and fall, to please the ear and eye, as well as to keep people cool in the heat. Jasmine, honeysuckle and roses are just a few of the many flowers the Moors brought to the region.

4 Philosophy

Great Andalucían minds, such as the Moor Averroës and the Jew Maimonides, were considered the foremost thinkers of their age. The former almost single-handedly preserved Aristotle's writings, while the latter's writings sought to reconcile biblical faith and reason.

5 Crafts

The hand-tooled leather of Córdoba, silver and gold filigree jewellery, pottery, silk and embroidered goods and inlaid creations all owe their existence to the Moors' 800-year rule.

6 Agriculture

Inheriting many of their techniques from the Romans, the Moors were expert agricultural engineers. Their system consisted of three main elements: the aqueduct, the waterwheel and the irrigation channel. Thereby, they were able to cultivate vast areas, often building ingenious terracing on slopes. They also introduced many crops, including bitter oranges, lemons, almonds, rice, cotton, asparagus and mulberry trees (to feed silkworms).

Rare Andalucían brass astrolabe

7 Science

Moorish scientists excelled in the fields of metallurgy, zoology, botany, medicine and mathematics. Inventors also developed revolutionary devices such as the astrolabe and the quadrant, both used for navigation. Arabic numerals were introduced by them, as well as algebra (from *al-jebr*, meaning "reuniting broken parts") and the algorithm.

8 Art and Architecture

Moorish art and architecture are full of signs and symbols and often incorporate calligraphy into their designs, quoting the Qur'an or poetry. The aim was to inspire reflection upon the unity of all things under Allah, whose power and perfection could never be equalled by human achievements.

9 Food

The simple fare that had existed prior to the Moorish incursion – centred around olives, wheat and grapes – gave way to flavours such as almonds, saffron, nutmeg, pepper and other spices.

10 Language

Modern Spanish language is full of everyday terms that come from Moorish heritage – *izquierda*, the word for "left", is almost pure Arabic, as is any word beginning with the prefix *al-* (the).

Terraced garden with pools at the Partal in the Alhambra

TOP 10 MOORISH SITES

1. Moorish Granada
The grand Alhambra palace *(p22)* is the crown jewel of Spain's Moorish heritage, while the nearby Generalife *(p24)* features lovely gardens.

2. Vejer de la Frontera
The architecture and design found in this village *(p112)* is the most Moorish of the *pueblos blancos*.

3. La Mezquita, Córdoba
With its stunning architecture, this mosque *(p32)* gave rise to the Arab-Hispanic style known as Caliphal.

4. Baños Árabes, Ronda
D5 Barrio de Padre Jesús
656 95 09 37
Three Moorish baths, the central one being the biggest, feature Arabic-style horseshoe arches.

5. Medina Azahara, Córdoba
This palace *(p131)* epitomized the city's splendour during the 10th century.

6. Almonaster la Real
This village's mosque is one of Andalucía's finest mosques *(p102)*, with great views from the minaret.

7. Real Alcázar, Seville
Seville's royal palace *(p28)* still features some of its Moorish origins, especially the front towers and the gateway to the palace.

8. Alcazaba, Málaga
In Málaga's Alcazaba *(p83)*, remains of the original Moorish walls and tower can still be seen, showcasing intricate Islamic design.

9. Las Alpujarras
F4
The villages on the slopes of the Sierra Nevada *(p44)* retain distinctive Moorish architecture, such as flat roofs and narrow winding alleys.

10. Alcazaba, Almería
G4 C/Almanzor s/n
950 80 10 08
Almeria's Alcazaba is one of the largest surviving Moorish fortresses in the region.

ASPECTS OF FLAMENCO

1 Origins
Flamenco has a rich and complex history. Undocumented until the 19th century, the dance is thought to derive from a blend of Arabic, Jewish and Roma cultures found in Andalucía. It is believed that the purest form of flamenco, known as *cante jondo*, originated from the geographical area between Cádiz, Jerez and Seville. According to Spanish folklorist Manuel García Matos, the word "flamenco" comes from a slang term meaning "flashy" or "ostentatious".

2 Dance
Flamenco dance is charged with intense passion and *duende* (a transcendent state of inspiration). While similarities between Middle Eastern and North African dance forms and flamenco are obvious, the rapid staccato rhythms, combined with expressive arm and hand gestures, clearly resemble traditional kathak dancing from northern India.

3 Song
Flamenco song is fervent, rhythmic music full of pathos and catharsis. It can be categorized into three types: *cante jondo*, a deeply emotional song of anguish and despair; *cante intermedio*, an "intermediate" song which combines elements of Spanish music styles; and *cante chico*, a light, joyful song that celebrates life.

4 Guitar
The six-stringed flamenco guitar can be traced back to the medieval lute. It is lighter, shallower and less resonant than a classical guitar, and can be played extremely fast. A plate below the sound hole is used for tapping out rhythms.

5 Cajón
In 1977, the renowned flamenco artist Paco de Lucía discovered the Peruvian *cajón* while on tour. A kind of box drum that creates a sound similar to that of a dancer's heel tapping the floor, it was incorporated into de Lucía's music and has become a staple of flamenco ever since.

6 Palmas and Pitos
Palmas (hand clapping) punctuates song and dance. There are two styles, *fuertes* (hard), which is used during louder pieces, and *sordas* (soft), for quieter accompaniment. *Pitos* (snapping fingers) can also mark the rhythm at specific moments.

7 Attire
Female flamenco costumes usually feature elaborate ruffles, fringed scarves and hair accessories, such as roses. Dresses with long, flouncy trains are called *bata de cola* and require special training

Flamenco performance at Plaza de España, Seville

to dance in. Male dancers often wear a waistcoat and dress shirt with fitted trousers and boots.

8 Sevillanas

Sevillanas originated as the Seguidilla dance, which still exists in the Castile region today. In the 19th century this strident dance was infused with flamenco spirit and became a popular folk dance now prevalent at Andalucían festivals. Sevillanas has four parts and is danced in pairs, with passing turns and elaborate arm and hand movements, accompanied by the guitar, *cajón*, castanets and clapping rhythms.

9 Performances

Flamenco can be enjoyed in a variety of venues, such as formal theatres, *tablaos* (upscale performance spaces) and even rustic cave settings, where you'll find well-choreographed, professional performances. For something more spontaneous, head to a *peña* (cultural association dedicated to flamenco) or an intimate flamenco bar.

10 Flamenco Legends

A few people who advanced the art include singers Camarón de la Isla, El Fillo and La Niña de los Peines; guitarist Paco de Lucía; and dancers La Macarrona and Carmen Amaya.

Legendary flamenco artist Paco de Lucía

TOP 10 FLAMENCO VENUES

1. Tablao El Arenal, Seville
Seville's most iconic flamenco venue, Tablao El Arenal *(p95)* is known for its top performances.

2. Peña La Bulería, Jerez de la Frontera
B5 C/Empedrada 20
640 71 85 21
This club is named after a fast flamenco style that originated in Jerez.

3. Museo de Baile Flamenco, Seville
B5 C/Manuel Rojas Marcos 3
museodelbaileflamenco.com
An interactive flamenco museum that also offers nightly performances.

4. Taberna Flamenca La Cava, Cádiz
B5 C/Antonio López 16, Cádiz flamencolacava.com
Enjoy flamenco in the setting of a traditional tavern.

5. Puro Arte, Jerez de la Frontera
B5 C/Madre de Dios 10, Jerez de la Frontera 660 03 04 20
Watch the best flamenco performed by acclaimed artists here – book ahead.

6. Casa de la Memoria de al-Andalus, Seville
A museum and flamenco cultural centre *(p95)*, set in a courtyard house, with nightly live performances.

7. Tablao Flamenco Cardenal, Córdoba
D3 C/Buen Pastor 2
tablaoflamencocardenal.es
Traditional flamenco music and dancing in an 18th-century manor.

8. Venta El Gallo, Granada
F4 Barranco de los Negros 5
cuevaventaelgallo.es
The Zambra style of flamenco is the highlight at Venta El Gallo.

9. La Peña Platería, Granada
F4 Placeta de Toqueros 7
laplateria.es
This is one of Spain's oldest *peñas*.

10. Teatro Flamenco, Málaga
T5 C/Lazcano 5
teatroflamencomalaga.com
One of the city's most vibrant spots, perfect for enjoying a flamenco show.

MUSEUMS AND GALLERIES

1 Sala Antiquarium, Seville

M2 Plaza de la Encarnación 955 47 15 80 10am–7:30pm daily (to 1:30pm Sun & public hols)

Below the extraordinary Metropol Parasol in Plaza de la Encarnación *(p93)* lies a hidden museum with fascinating archaeological remains found in 1973, when the Parasol complex was being built. Extensive Roman ruins date from the Tiberius era onwards (around 30–600 CE) and there is a Moorish house dating back to the 12th–13th centuries.

2 Museo Picasso, Málaga

E5 C/San Agustín 8 10am–7pm daily museopicassomalaga.org

This is the world's third-largest museum dedicated to Picasso, the modern master. It honours his wish for his native city to be a part of his artistic legacy. With over 187 paintings, the collection here covers eight decades of the artist's career and gives an idea of the breadth and depth of Picasso's work.

3 Museo Automovilistico y de la Moda, Málaga

E5 Avda Sor Teresa Prat 15 10am–2:30pm & 4–7pm daily museoautomovilmoda.com

This museum has an excellent private collection of classic cars from designers like Bugatti, Figoni, Firestone and Labourdette. There is also a section dedicated to *haute couture.*

Vintage car, Museo Automovilistico

Painted domed ceiling of the Museo de Bellas Artes, Seville

4 Museo de Bellas Artes, Seville

Housed in an exquisite former convent, this art museum *(p90)* is second only to Madrid's famed Prado. Paintings include early works by Velázquez, and important pieces by Zurbarán, Ribera, El Greco, Murillo, Valdés Leal and Vásquez.

5 Museo Provincial de Jaén

E3 Paseo de la Estación 29 9am–9pm Tue–Sun museosdeandalucia.es

The lower floor of this museum contains some truly extraordinary 5th-century BCE Iberian stone sculptures. Found near the town of Porcuna, in the western part of the province, the exhibits on display show clear influences from Greek works. Upstairs, the museum also has some fine medieval wood sculpture.

6 Centre Pompidou, Málaga

V5 Pasaje Doctor Carrillo Casaux 9:30am–8pm Wed–Mon centrepompidou-malaga.eu

An offshoot of the Parisian art museum, this museum has rare pieces and features artists like Francis Bacon, Frida Kahlo, René Magritte and Pablo Picasso. Exhibits are divided thematically.

7 Museo Municipal, Antequera

D4 Palacio Nájera, Plaza del Coso Viejo 10am–6pm daily museoantequera.es

Housed in a grand 18th-century ducal palace, this museum has an excellent collection of Roman archaeological and ethnological exhibits. Highlights include the life-size 1st-century CE Roman bronze representing a naked young man, possibly Ganymede, cupbearer to the gods, and a lifelike carving of St Francis of Assisi in wood by Pedro de Mena, a 17th-century Andalucían master.

8 Museo de Cádiz

B5 Plaza de Mina 956 00 81 50 9am–9pm Tue–Sat, 9am–3pm Sun & public hols

Located in a Neo-Classical mansion, this museum has treasures from the city's ancient civilizations and an impressive fine art collection. The notable exhibit is a pair of marble sarcophagi dating to the 5th century BCE. Among the art are works by Zurbarán, Rubens, Murillo and Cano. An ethnological collection has pieces that highlight aspects of the city's culture. Entry is free for EU citizens.

9 Museo Arqueológico, Córdoba

D3 Plaza Jerónimo Páez 7 957 35 55 17 9am–9pm Tue–Sat, 9am–3pm Sun, public hols & in summer

In a small 16th-century Renaissance mansion, this museum has an excellent collection that highlights the city's importance in Roman times. In fact, it was built over a Roman structure and an ancient patio proves it. A sculpture of the Persian god Mithras, found at Cabra, is particularly fine. The collection also focuses on Iberian finds and Moorish artifacts.

10 Parque de las Ciencias, Granada

This dazzling science park *(p122)* has many interactive exhibitions on such topics as the human body, outer space, the environment and technology.

Exploring exhibits at the Parque de las Ciencias, Granada

ART AND CULTURAL FIGURES

***A King of Spain* (c 1645) by Alonso Cano**

1 Alonso Cano

Architect, painter and sculptor, Granada-born Alonso Cano (1601–67) studied art and began his illustrious career in Seville before moving to Madrid, where King Philip IV appointed him as royal architect and painter. He later returned to Granada, where most of his works can be seen today.

2 Andrés de Vandelvira

Andrés de Vandelvira (1509–75) was the quintessential architect of the Spanish Renaissance in Andalucía. His work spanned the three major phases of the style's predominance, from ornamental Plateresque, to Italianate Classical, to austere Herrerean. He can virtually be given sole credit for the architectural treasures in the town of Úbeda, as well as for many of the most important Renaissance edifices in nearby Baeza *(p40)*.

3 Bartolomé Esteban Murillo

Bartolomé Esteban Murillo (1618–82) was one of the most successful of the Baroque painters from Seville. He received countless commissions to produce devotional works, notably the many *Immaculate Conceptions* seen in Andalucía.

4 María Zambrano

María Zambrano (1904–91), born in Vélez-Málaga, was a pioneering philosopher known for incorporating *razón poética* (poetic reason) into her work. Deeply influenced by Andalucían culture, her intellectual contributions earned her Spain's prestigious Cervantes Prize and cemented her legacy in philosophy.

5 Luisa Roldán

Luisa Roldán (1652–1706), known as La Roldana, was Spain's first documented female sculptor. After creating works for Cádiz Cathedral, she became court sculptor to kings Charles II and Philip V. Though influenced by her father, the renowned sculptor Pedro Roldán, Luisa's legacy shines as a trailblazer in Spanish Baroque sculpture.

6 Federico García Lorca

The Granada-born poet and playwright (1898–1936) was also an artist, musician and theatre director. Due to his sexuality and Socialist views, he was murdered by Franco's Nationalists at the start of the Spanish Civil War. His work shows his love for Andalucían culture.

7 Pablo Picasso

Pablo Picasso (1881–1973) was born in Málaga, although he settled in France in 1909. His native land, with images of the bullfight and later of the horrors of the Franco era, featured in his work throughout his career.

Zurbarán's *The Apparition of Saint Peter to Saint Peter Nolasco* (1629)

8 Francisco de Zurbarán

Zurbarán (1598–1664) spent most of his life in and around Seville, where his art adorns many churches and museums. His works are noted for their mystical qualities, dramatized by striking *chiaroscuro* (light and shade) effects.

9 Manuel de Falla

Andalucían-born de Falla (1876–1946) was Spain's finest classical composer. One of his major works, *The Three-Cornered Hat*, has its roots deep in flamenco.

10 Diego Rodríguez de Silva y Velázquez

Born in Seville, Velázquez (1599–1660) left for Madrid in 1623 to become court painter to the king. A remarkable talent of his time, he took naturalism to new heights. The works that remain in his hometown now are mostly religious commissions; however, his real genius lay in portraits.

Famous Spanish painter Diego Velázquez

TOP 10 WORKS INSPIRED BY ANDALUCÍA

1. The Marriage of Figaro (1786)
Mozart's famed opera is set in Seville, during the late 18th century, and takes place over the course of a single day.

2. Don Juan (1819)
English Romantic poet Lord Byron's fascination with Andalucía is chronicled in this famous work.

3. Tales of the Alhambra (1832)
American writer Washington Irving lived in Granada for some time and produced this hit collection of essays, sketches and stories inspired by his stay here.

4. Andalusían Scenes (1847)
Málaga-born writer Serafín Estébanez Calderón included the first literary description of a Roma festival in this influential 19th-century work.

5. Cante Jondo (1912)
Many of Antonio Machado's works, including *Cante Jondo*, evoke a poetic passion for Andalucía.

6. Un Chien Andalou (1929)
This avant-garde film was created by the Surrealist pair Salvador Dalí and Luis Buñuel.

7. For Whom the Bell Tolls (1940)
This literary classic by American writer Ernest Hemingway was inspired by his experiences in Andalucía during Spain's Civil War.

8. The Moor's Last Sigh (1995)
This novel by Indian-born British-American author Salman Rushdie was inspired by the exile of Granada's last Moorish king.

9. Driving Over Lemons (1999)
Former Genesis drummer Chris Stewart wrote this fascinating memoir about relocating to a lovely Andalucían farmhouse.

10. Factory of Light (2003)
Written by Michael Jacobs, this book is a vivid, witty and informative account of his experiences and encounters in the Andalucían village of Frailes, near Jaén.

VILLAGES

1 Almonaster la Real

From a distance, this lovely *pueblo blanco* in Huelva Province looks like a sprinkling of snow amid the green of the surrounding forests. The citadel here *(p102)* features one of the oldest mosques in the region, dating from the 10th century.

2 Alájar

Set against the dramatic rocky outcrop of Peña de Arias Montano, Alájar *(p102)* is one of the prettiest villages in Huelva Province. It is home to stone houses, Baroque churches and intriguing hallowed caves. At its heart is a 16th-century chapel, which is a popular local pilgrimage site.

3 El Rocío

Deserted for the majority of the year, except for its handful of residents – who still customarily get around on horseback – this town *(p99)* overflows with around one million pilgrims during the annual *romería (p84)*. It's worth a visit at any time to take in its wonderful Wild West-style architecture, as well as to book a tour of the nearby Parque Nacional de Doñana *(p42)*.

4 Vejer de la Frontera

This inland village *(p112)* in Cádiz Province probably retains its quintessential Moorish character more than any other village or town in Andalucía. It stands gleaming white on a steep hill with a stunning view of the coast, and its maze-like alleys and byways are virtually indistinguishable from any North African town. Before the Spanish Civil War, women here wore a traditional veiled garment like the Islamic hijab, called the *cobijado*; now this traditional attire is only worn during the August festival.

5 Arcos de la Frontera

The historic part of Arcos de la Frontera *(p110)* stretches from the Cuesta de Belén to the Puerta de Matrera. This area has been a beautifully preserved national monument since 1962. Its labyrinth of narrow streets invites exploration on foot. At it's centre is the Plaza del Cabildo, with ancient walls towering above rows of orange trees. While, the castle below the square remains closed to the public, the terrace of the parador opposite is open and offers a wonderful spot to enjoy a drink with a beautiful view.

6 Zahara de la Sierra

C4

The town's name means "flower" in Arabic and this quiet little hamlet, scented with orange groves, lives up to its reputation. It's a delight to see on the approach and offers fine views once there. The ruined castle, however, stands witness to tougher times. In the 15th century it was attacked continually, sought by both Muslims and Christians for its position guarding the access route to the Serranía de Ronda *(p75)*.

7 Iznatoraf

F2

This mountain eyrie of a place opens out onto 360-degree panoramas of the Cazorla highland. The best view is from the mirador above the cliff at the village's northern edge.

8 Cazorla

G3

Simple whitewashed cubes cluster around a citadel here, while birds of prey overhead remind you that this is the southwestern entrance to the Sierra de Cazorla *(p66)*. The town's strategic position attracted both Moors and Christians, hence there's a castle in the town and the ruined La Iruela is just 1 km (half a mile) away.

Buildings lining a pretty cobbled street in Castril

9 Castril

G3

At the foot of an imposing stone outcrop and surrounded by the Parque Natural de la Sierra de Castril, this enchanting town dates back to Roman times. A mountain torrent surges below the idyllic setting.

10 Sabiote

F2

This hidden gem is known for its remarkably well-preserved medieval walls. It is home to one of the most impressive castles in the region. Originally of Moorish origin, the castle was later restored by the famed architect Andrés de Vandelvira, who was born here.

Castillo de la Yedra overlooking the town of Cazorla

Pilgrims dressed in traditional attire during the vibrant Romería del Rocío

CRISTINA

PASEOS, PLAZAS, PARKS AND GARDENS

Domed gazebo at the Jardin Botánico la Concepción, Málaga

1 Jardín Botánico la Concepción, Málaga

E5 Ctra N331 km 166
9:30am–5:30pm Tue–Sun (Apr–Sep: to 8:30pm) laconcepcion.malaga.eu

This impressive botanical garden is the work of a 19th-century English woman, Amalia Livermore, and her Spanish husband, Jorge Loring Oyarzábal. It has a collection of palms and plants from around the world. The grounds also have charming touches, such as a domed gazebo decorated with tiles and columns. Visitors can stay here for half an hour after the closing time.

2 Plaza San Juan de Dios, Cádiz

B5

This is one of Cádiz's busiest hubs of commercial and social life. Lined with cafés, bars and palm trees, its chief adornment is the monumental Neo-Classical façade of the Ayuntamiento (town hall), with its several handsome towers. The square opens out onto the port, ensuring a constant stream of pedestrians and great opportunities for hours of people-watching.

3 Parque Genovés, Cádiz

B5 Av. Dr. Gómez Ulla, s/n

This stretch of landscaped greenery overlooking the sea features strolling paths, some civic sculptures and riveting flora, including an ancient dragon tree from the Canary Islands. It forms one part of a two-section park; the other half curving along the northern seafront.

4 Jardín Botánico La Almunya del Sur, Almeria

G5 Paraje Tarambana 284
10am–2pm & 5–8pm Wed–Sat, 10am–2pm Sun laalmunyadelsur.es

This botanical garden has over 1,600 types of plants across biodiverse spaces. Fruit and ornamental trees, shrubs, vines, succulents and colourful flowers line the walkways, where you'll find water features and shaded areas to relax. It is advisable to book your visit in advance.

5 Paseo Alcalde Marqués de Contadero, Seville

This central promenade *(p93)* is one of Seville's finest. Stretching along the riverfront, within sight of most of the

Tree-lined path at the Alcázar de los Reyes Cristianos, Córdoba

major monuments, its tree-lined walkways make a pleasant break from the crowded city streets. The *paseo* is also pedestrianized so you don't have to worry about traffic as you stroll.

6 Plaza de la Corredera, Córdoba

D3

Córdoba gave this 17th-century arcaded square a long overdue sprucing up for the tourist onslaught of 1992, even putting in an underground car park. But it still retains some of its customary functions, including an open-air market on Saturday morning, in addition to the regular market in the building with the clock tower. The arches provide shade for cafés and tapas bars, from where you can admire the brick façades with wrought-iron balconies.

7 Parque de María Luisa, Seville

Seville's glorious main park *(p93)* was a gift to the city from a Bourbon duchess in 1893. It was redesigned for the 1929 Ibero-American Exhibition. Many lavish structures have been left behind, including the stunning Plaza de España and several other fine buildings, two of which house local museums. The grounds are largely the creation of Jean-Claude Nicolas Forestier, the French landscape gardener who also designed the Bois de Boulogne in Paris.

8 Plaza Nueva, Granada

T2

Located at the base of the Alhambra hill and Albaicín *(p124)*, with great views along the river that runs beneath the city, this is a great place to while away the time. There are street performers, and plenty of cafés with outdoor seating.

9 Paseo de la Constitución, Baeza

F2

Built in the 16th century, this oblong central promenade is Baeza's main hub for strollers and café-goers. Fountains grace its tree-lined length, and there are bars with shady seating. Interesting buildings by the square include La Alhóndiga, the former corn exchange.

10 Alcázar de los Reyes Cristianos, Córdoba

D3 Campo Santo de los Mártires Hours vary, check website museosdecordoba.sacatuentrada.es

This palace-fortress dates back to the 14th century. Its lavish Moorish gardens indulge in a slew of colour setting off the sun-bleached stone walls and ancient carvings. Another nearby attraction is the 10th-century Baños del Alcázar Califal *(p30)*, an Arab bathhouse with the classical order of Roman baths: cold, warm and hot rooms.

NATURE RESERVES

1 Parque Nacional de la Sierra Nevada

F4 Ctra A 395 – dirección Pradollano – km 23, 18196 Güéjar Sierra 958 98 02 46

Spain's highest mainland mountains and Europe's southernmost ski resort can be found in this national park *(p44)*. It's a wonderful area for hiking, horse riding and mountain biking.

2 Sierra de Aracena y Picos de Aroche Park

This part *(p102)* of the Sierra Morena in Huelva Province is rural in character; traditions cling tighter here, notably the culinary techniques that give rise to its world-famous ham, *jamón ibérico*. The forested hills lend themselves to exploration on foot *(p72)*.

3 Sierra de Cazorla

G2

In eastern Jaén Province, this vast and enormously diverse park is home to some 1,300 known species of flora, including 20 that are unique to the zone. Steep cliffs, deep gorges and an intricate pattern of rivers, lakes and streams dominate the terrain. The area offers plenty of walking opportunities.

4 Sierra Norte

C3

Sevilla Province's northern reaches are wild and beautiful. Hiking is often a better option than driving, due to rough, pot-holed roads. A great choice for outdoor enthusiasts of any sort – anglers, hunters and climbers are in their element here.

5 Parque Nacional de Doñana

These floodplains *(p42)* are a UNESCO Biosphere Reserve and have been a national park since 1969, though its status is increasingly under threat due to ecological issues. More than six million birds stop here during their migrations and fauna includes the endangered Iberian lynx.

6 Cabo de Gata-Níjar

H4

In Almería Province, a stretch of pristine coastline has been preserved as a nature reserve, where towering rocks set off pretty beaches and coves. The semi-desert massif was designated a UNESCO Biosphere Reserve in 1997 and offers excellent scuba-diving opportunities.

Wild mountain goats, El Torcal de Antequera

7 El Torcal de Antequera

A popular spot for hikers and climbers, El Torcal de Antequera *(p112)* is Málaga Province's most dramatic natural landmark. This limestone massif, shaped by the weather over countless millennia, features surreal formations.

8 Sierra de Grazalema

C5

A huge expanse of verdant wilderness was designated a UNESCO Biosphere Reserve in 1977. Access is strictly controlled and is only possible on foot.

9 Parque Natural de la Sierra de Cardeña y Montoro

E2

This beautiful park is home to forests of holm oak, cork and pine. For the most part gently rolling, it gives way to more dramatic terrain in the west. There are plenty of hiking trails and places to spot local fauna.

10 Parque Natural de los Montes de Málaga

E5

Most of this park was planted to cover Málaga's once-barren hills so as to prevent the seasonal flooding the city experienced for several centuries. Just 30 minutes from town, it's an excellent place for hiking and biking, with colour-coded trails.

Hiking amid vibrant greenery in the Sierra de Cazorla

TOP 10 FLORA AND FAUNA

1. Marsh Birds
The watery areas are abound with cranes, flamingos, wild ducks, gull-billed terns, purple gallinules, stilts, glossy ibis and redshanks.

2. Shrubs
Along the coast you'll see agave, brought here from America in the 18th century, as well as prickly pear, bull- rush, club rush, oleander and arbutus. Spanish lavender, an aromatic shrub, is also common.

3. Wild Flowers
Look for the Cazorla violet, bubil lily, Nevada daffodil, white celandine and narrow-leaved biarum.

4. Raptors
Birds of prey found here include the Spanish imperial eagle, the golden eagle, the griffon vulture and the peregrine falcon.

5. Songbirds
Listen carefully for the red-legged partridge, collared pratincole and hoopoe, named for its distinctive "hoop-hoop-hoop" call.

6. Trees
Here, you will find trees like black and umbrella pine, holm oak, hazel, olive, citrus, cypress, juniper and ash. As well as the rare Spanish fir, the national tree of Andalucía.

7. Mammals
Wild creatures include wolves, lynxes, boars, genets, mongoose, monk seals, dolphins, whales and the Barbary macaques of Gibraltar, the only wild monkey population in Europe.

8. Reptiles and Amphibians
This group includes the Montpellier snake, the Spanish lizard and the natterjack toad.

9. Fish
Local catch includes black perch, eels, gambusia, tuna, monkfish, sardines, anchovies and cephalopods.

10. Insects and Arachnids
Most of Europe's butterflies can be found here, along with mosquitoes, scorpions and tarantulas.

BEACHES

1 Chipiona

Cádiz Province features several beach resorts that offer quiet stays and a range of activities along the coast, with Chipiona *(p112)* standing out as one of the most charming spots. The beaches are excellent and the town has retained its age-old traditions. It's still a thriving fishing port, for example, as well as a renowned producer of the local sweet muscatel wine. In addition, historic attractions include the longest jetty in the Guadalquivir estuary, known as Turris Caepionis to the Romans and these days as Torre Scipio.

2 Tarifa

Tarifa *(p112)*, Cádiz Province's – and mainland Europe's – southernmost point, is one of the world's best destinations for enjoying the west wind. The wind rarely ceases blowing here, making it perfect for kite- and windsurfing, though less ideal for sunbathers. Still, it is possible to find protected niches that shelter you from the wind, and the nightlife and sense of fun here are second to none.

3 Mazagón

B4

Huelva Province's Costa de la Luz has several appealingly remote beaches, and Mazagón is one of them. Located 23 km (14 miles) southeast of Huelva, this low-key resort is surrounded by pines and has lovely dune beaches. Deserted in winter, it comes alive in summer, mostly with families, but there's plenty of empty expanse to find solitude.

Lighthouse at Playa de Chipiona in Cádiz

Historic town of Nerja, overlooking the sea

4 Nerja
E5

This lovely town is a favourite among those seeking panoramic Mediterranean views away from the holiday crowds. It's a welcoming spot, with a wonderful position on top of an imposing cliff with palm-fringed beaches below.

5 Almuñécar

The main resort (p122) on the Costa Tropical of Granada Province is a more relaxed alternative to the intensity of the Costa del Sol. The two central beaches are the Playa San Cristóbal and the Playa Puerto del Mar, separated by a headland. Good diving and windsurfing spots can be found along here.

6 Torre del Mar
E5

This area is frequented by families and has vast sandy beaches as well as a waterpark nearby.

7 Marbella
D5

This town naturally has several fine beaches to explore. To the east there is Cabo Pino, a nudist beach, and Las Dunas, known for its sand dunes and marina. To the west is a string of party beaches, perfect for barbecues and dancing, including the famous Nikki beach.

8 Torremolinos
E5

Torremolinos is home to several pleasant beaches, but due to the area's steep streets, most of the recreational activities take place uphill.

9 Ayamonte
A4

Andalucía's westernmost town, Ayamonte, is located at the mouth of Río Guadiana. To the east are the beach resorts of Isla Canela and Isla Cristina. Isla Canela features a long, broad beach and an array of bars serving well-crafted cocktails, while Isla Cristina has a fine sandy stretch and a harbour.

10 Cabo de Gata
H5

Cabo de Gata in Almería Province offers some of the region's finest unspoiled beaches, including the Cala de la Media Luna and the Playa de Mónsul. The main resort town in this natural park (p66) is San José.

OUTDOOR ACTIVITIES AND SPORTS

1 Hiking

Andalucía's sierras range from verdant to desert-like and rocky, and are perfect for hiking. If mountaineering appeals, head for the Sierra Nevada *(p44)*. Maps and lists of refuges are available from the Federación Andaluza de Montañismo or FEDAMON *(fadmes.es)*.

2 Horse Riding

Renowned for its tradition of breeding fine horses, Andalucía offers a range of riding options, with scenic trails and riding schools spread across every province. Riding Fun in the Sun *(ridingfuninthesun.com)* provides tours in English through the lovely countryside of Málaga, while Caballos y Vino *(caballosyvino.com)* offers horse-back riding packages across Ronda.

3 Windsurfing and Surfing

Tarifa is a hot spot for windsurfing, while the Costa Tropical also offers excellent conditions. The Costa de la Luz has strong waves perfect for surfing, while the Mediterranean waves are ideal for body-boarding and SUP (stand-up paddleboarding). Laduna Tarifa *(tarifawindsurfing.com)* and Windsurf La Herradura *(windsurflaherradura.com)* both offer a wide range of surfing activities for all levels.

4 Spelunking

The region has some of the world's most interesting caves, many of which are open to the public. Team4you *(team4you.es)* offers tours led by experienced guides. Natur Sport Sorbas in Almería *(cuevasdesorbas.com)* has many routes for all levels, with guides available in Spanish, English, French and German.

5 Skiing

The frosty peaks of the Sierra Nevada (p44) are perfect for winter sports. Although a little too sleek compared to its Alpine cousins, it offers a variety of runs and, best of all, the chance to ski well into the off season.

6 Boating and Fishing

Sailing is big in this part of Spain. For deep-sea and freshwater fishing, you will need to obtain a licence. Check the Andalucían Fishing Federation *(fapd.org)*, Andalucían Sailing Federation *(fav.es)* and Ports and Logistics Areas of Andalucía *(puertosdeandalucia.es)* websites for more details.

7 Golf

So copious are the golf courses that the Costa del Sol has often been dubbed the "Costa del Golf". Courses range from

world masterpieces, designed by top golfers, to putting greens suitable for families. Valderrama *(valderrama.com)* and Real Club de Golf Sotogrande *(golf sotogrande.com)* are two of the most famous.

8 Diving

The waters off Gibraltar are dotted with sunken ships, while Cabo de Gata boasts some of the richest marine life in the region. For basic or speciality diving courses, check out Centro de Buceo Isub *(isubsanjose.com)*. Along the Costa de la Luz, there are excellent dive spots, especially near Tarifa. Yellow Sub Tarifa *(divingtarifa.com)* organizes diving trips and PADI diving courses here.

9 Football

A national obsession, *fútbol* (football) stirs up the deepest of passions in Spain. In season, you will find matches being shown in every bar, blaring out from the TV, watched by animated locals.

10 Hot-Air Ballooning

Soar through the peaceful morning skies in a hot-air balloon, enjoying views of the picturesque Andalucían countryside. Both Globotur *(globotur.es)* and Glovento Sur *(gloventosur.com)* offer hot-air balloon flights across the region.

Windsurfing in Tarifa, Costa de la Luz

TOP 10 BIKE ROUTES

1. Via Verde El Ronquillo, Sevilla
B3
A pleasant 9-km (5.6-mile) route running along the Minilla reservoir.

2. Via Verde del Sierra Norte, Sevilla
C3
Ride 15 km (9.3 miles) along the Ribera del Huéznar river to Cerro del Hierro.

3. Via Verde del Riotinto, Huelva
B3–A4
A 35-km (21.7-mile) trail through hilly scrublands and Riotinto's Martian terrain.

4. Via Verde del Subbética, Córdoba
E3
Starting from Luque, take in castles and caves in a 57-km (35.4-mile) trail.

5. Via Verde del Aceite, Jaén
E3
Ride through rolling hills and olive groves on this 55-km (34.2-mile) route.

6. Via Verde Sierra de Baza, Granada
G3
Pass meadows and the village of Baza on this 16-km (9.9-mile) ride to Caniles.

7. Via Verde del Entre Rios, Cádiz
B4–B5
Explore farmlands and dunes along the Atlantic coast in a 16-km (9.9-mile) ride.

8. Via the TransAndalus, Cádiz
C6–B5
This 341-km (211.8-mile) route is best experienced on a mountain bike.

9. Via the TransAndalus, Málaga
C5–E4
Climb through mountains and take in stunning gorges on this 214-km (132.9-mile) bike route.

10. Villanueva del Rosario, Málaga
D4–E4
This is a 19-km (11.8-mile) child-friendly route from Camino de las Huertas.

Walking along the Vereda de la Estrella trail, in the Sierra Nevada

HIKES AND DRIVES

Winding road leading to the Castillo Almodóvar del Rio

1 Drive through Guadalquivir Valley, Córdoba Province

E2

Starting to the east of Córdoba, in the attractive hill town of Montoro, then follow the river downstream. To the west of Córdoba, visit the fabulous Medina Azahara *(p131)*, enjoy the view from Almodóvar del Río's castle walls and end the drive at Palma del Río.

2 Drive from Nerja to Almería

E5 Rte N340

This route takes you along some of the region's most panoramic coastline. Nerja, perched atop cliffs *(p69)*, offers great views and as you approach Almería *(p122)* the landscape becomes even more dramatic.

3 Drive from Tarifa to Cádiz

C6 Rte N340

With its imposing cliffs and mammoth sand dunes, this wild sweep of the Costa de la Luz *(p111)* offers one of the most spectacular drives along the Atlantic coast. The village of Bolonia, with its Roman ruins, and Vejer de la Frontera *(p112)*, which is steeped in Moorish heritage, make for excellent side trips.

4 Drive from Ronda to Jerez

D5 Rte N342

The main attraction are the *pueblos blancos (p109)*, particularly Grazalema, Zahara and Arcos de la Frontera, as well as the Roman ruins at Ronda la Vieja.

5 Drive in Las Alpujarras, Sierra Nevada

F4

Begin at Lanjarón *(p45)*, then head for Órgiva. Continuing eastwards, you will come to Yegen, made famous by Gerald Brenan's *South from Granada.*

6 Hike around the Villages of the Southern Tahá

F4

This hike descends south from Pitres to Mecinilla, then along a ravine to Mecina-Fondales. From here, take the short or long route to Ferreirola, climb up to Atalbéitar and then head back to Pitres.

7 Hike from Alájar to Linares de la Sierra

B3

The Sierra de Aracena is defined by soaring cliffs, wooded valleys and villages. A good 6-km (4-mile) hike along marked trails leads from Alájar

Strolling along a trail in the lush Sierra de Aracena

to Linares, via the hamlet of Los Madroñeros. From Alájar's main square, it follows the old road, with only one steep section.

8 Hike from Rute to Iznájar

E4

Start in Rute and head south on the A331, veer left at the fork and then take the trail on the right about 500 m (550 yd) further on. This leads down to the reservoir; turn right and continue to a rocky promontory. Enjoy the views here, then go up the hill and cross the bridge to the scenic village of Iznájar.

9 Serranía de Ronda Hike

D5

A picturesque hike connects the village of Benaoján Estación with Jimera de Líbar Estación. Begin at the Molino del Santo hotel, then walk down the hill alongside the railway. Across the river is the path; take the left fork here and continue on Via Pecuaria to town.

10 Río Borosa Hike

G2

From the visitors' centre at the village of Torre del Vinagre, near Cazorla *(p61)*, this hike takes you along the narrow rock walls of the Cerrada de Elías gorge above the Río Borosa, criss crossed by wooden bridges.

TOP 10 TOWN AND CITY WALKS

Córdoba's Jewish quarter

1. Córdoba
Wander around the ancient Jewish quarter and then head for the Puente Romano for stunning sunset views *(p30)*.

2. Granada
Explore a maze of hilly streets in the Albaicín district *(p124)*.

3. Seville
Once you've explored the city-centre sights, head across the Puente de Isabel II and into the old working class quarter of Triana *(p92)*.

4. Cádiz
Start at the northeast corner of Plaza de España and stroll around the city, taking in the lovely seascapes and gardens *(p34)*.

5. Jerez de la Frontera
Visit the capital of sherry production and tour one of its bodegas *(p110)*.

6. Ronda
Cross the Puente Nuevo and follow the town clockwise, taking in the façade of the main church *(p36)*.

7. Baeza
From Plaza del Pópulo most of the sights are found within walking distance *(p40)*.

8. Úbeda
Take a westerly walk to the monumental Hospital de Santiago and the Plaza de Toros *(p40)*.

9. Málaga
Enjoy a tour of Málaga's historic sights north of the Paseo del Parque *(p108)*.

10. Antequera
This ancient town's main attractions are at the foot of the Alcazaba. Visitors can also enjoy the views from high above *(p108)*.

FAMILY ATTRACTIONS

Limestone formations at the Cuevas de Nerja

1 Cuevas de Nerja

E5 Ctra Maro 9:30am–4:30pm daily (Jul & Aug: to 7pm) 1 Jan & 15 May cuevadenerja.es

Discovered in 1959, these caves date back some five million years. The lighting here highlights the features of each cavern, from shadows to waterfalls. The central column in Cataclysm Hall is the tallest in the world.

2 Muelle de las Carabelas, La Rábida, Huelva

A4 Paraje de La Rábida Mid-Jun–mid-Sep: 10am–9pm Tue–Sun; Mid-Sep–mid-Jun: 9:30am–7:30pm Tue–Sun 1 & 6 Jan; 24, 25 & 31 Dec muelledelascarabelasentradas.com

Down by the waterfront, the "Pier of the Caravels" is a great treat for kids. Here, they can explore the full-sized replicas of Christopher Columbus's ships, *La Niña, La Pinta* and *La Santa María*. There's also a small museum and a re-creation of a 15th-century European village.

3 El Parque Minero de Ríotinto, Huelva

Explore 3,000 years of mining and railway history at this museum's *(p99)* reconstructed Roman mine. The museum offers a unique mix of history, geology and industrial heritage. Visitors can hop on board the Rio Tinto Express for a 12-km (7.5-mile) ride through the landscape, featuring old locomotives and mining equipment.

Enjoying a boat ride at the popular Isla Mágica, Seville

4 Carromato de Max, Mijas

D5 Avda del Compás 10am–2pm daily carromatodemijas.org

This oddball collection claims to be a compendium of the world's smallest curiosities. There's a fine copy of Da Vinci's *The Last Supper* executed on a grain of rice, fleas in suits and Churchill's head sculpted in chalk.

5 Parque de las Ciencias, Granada

This fascinating science centre and museum *(p122)* features a planetarium and a biodome holding more than 200 species of flora and fauna. With regular exhibitions, mechanical games, workshops and optical shows, it's sure to delight and pique curious minds of all ages.

6 Aventura Amazonia, Marbella

D5 Avda Valeriano Rodríguez 2 Hours vary, check website aventura-amazonia.com

Aventura Amazonia is the largest adventure park in Andalucía, with 103 challenges, 24 ziplines and a daring 12 m (40 ft) "Monkey Jump". The activities are suitable for children over the age of four. Safety briefings and harnesses are provided to ensure a safe experience for all participants.

7 Mini Hollywood, Almería

G4 Ctra N340 km 464, Tabernas Hours vary, check website minihollywoodoasys.com

The Wild West rides again at this old "spaghetti western" movie set. At show time, kids can see Jesse James in action.

8 Aqua Tropic, Almuñécar

F5 Playa de Velilla, Paseo Reina Sofia Mid-Jun–Sep: 11am–7pm daily aqua-tropic.com

Perfect for a hot summer day, this water park offers fun for all ages with thrilling rides like Kamikazee, Wave-breaker, Ring Rapids, Blackhole Rapids, Soft Runs, plus a lake for the little ones.

9 Parque Acuático Vera

H4 Avda Ciudad de Valencia, Vera Mid-May–Jun & Sep: 11am–6pm daily; Jul & Aug: 11am–7:30pm daily aquavera.com

This water park is a popular spot for both visitors and locals on hot summer days. It features five pools of varying sizes and plenty of slides and tubes.

10 Isla Mágica, Seville

K1 Pabellón España, Isla de Cartuja Hours vary, check website islamagica.es

This amusement park re-creates the exploits of the 16th-century explorers who set out on expeditions. It has a wide range of exciting rides with names like Jaguar and Anaconda. There are also boat tours and musical performances through the day.

LOCAL DISHES

Delicious serving of *fritura de pescado*

1 Calamares

Along the coast, grilled whole baby *calamares* (squid) is quite a popular dish. Fresh squid can also be cut into rings and batter-fried, offering a sweet and tender taste. A full serving of *fritura de pescado* or *fritura mixta* (mixed fried fish) may also include anchovies, prawns, cod chunks or other fresh catches of the day.

2 Tortilla Española and Patatas Bravas

Both of these dishes are popular not just in Andalucía but throughout Spain. A hearty potato and onion omelette, fried into a savoury cake, *tortilla española* is served cold, by the slice, and is so filling it can be a full meal. In contrast, *patatas bravas* consists of fried potato wedges served with a spicy tomato sauce and mayonnaise.

3 Fish Soups

Andalucía is known for its variety of *sopas de mariscos* (shellfish soups) and *sopas de pescado* (fish soups). In Málaga, favourites include *sopa viña*, a sherry-spiked version, and *cachoreñas*, with orange flavouring. Cádiz, on the other hand, is famous for its *guisos marineros* (seafood stews), made with the seasonal fish of the region.

4 Gazpacho

A signature Andalucían dish, this refreshing cold soup is ideal for a light lunch. It is usually made with fresh tomatoes, green peppers, cucumber, garlic, olive oil and breadcrumbs, and is seasoned with salt and either wine vinegar or lemon. There are dozens of local variations of this nourishing soup, which may involve almonds, grapes, melon, strawberries, red peppers, boiled egg or ham garnishes.

5 Arroz a la Marinera

The Andalucían version of paella, *arroz a la marinera* is also known as *arroz con mariscos*. This saffron-flavoured rice dish features a variety of seafood, including prawns, clams and squid. However, unlike the Valencian version, it does not include sausage or chicken. Instead, it focuses on the fresh, briny flavours of the sea. The dish is often finished with a touch of olive oil and fresh parsley for extra aroma and depth.

Traditional Spanish dessert *tocino de cielo*

6 Tocino de Cielo

This rich egg custard pudding was traditionally made by nuns in Jerez de la Frontera.

7 Monkfish

Monkfish *(rape)*, also called anglerfish, is one of the top choices for maritime eating in Andalucía. Only the tail of this fish is eaten, and it has a succulent quality similar to lobster tail or scallops. It is usually grilled, but can also be stewed in a rich, tomato-based sauce.

8 Salads

Andalucían *ensaladas* (salads) often include asparagus, boiled eggs, artichoke, carrots, olives, tuna and onions, in addition to lettuce and tomato.

9 Valle de los Pedroches

Preserved in olive oil and enhanced with herbs, this soft sheep's cheese from Córdoba Province is quite strong in taste.

10 Dessert Tarts

Cakes and sweet biscuits typically involve Moorish ingredients such as anise, sesame and cinnamon. Most are sweetened with honey rather than sugar. Two common types are *alfajores*, with honey and almonds, and *piononos*, sometimes soaked in liqueur.

***Arroz a la marinera* with shellfish**

TOP 10 TAPAS DISHES

1. Ensaladilla
Also known as "Russian salad", this dish features diced vegetables usually mixed with mayonnaise, sometimes including cubes of ham.

2. Chorizo al Vino
These spicy pork sausages, flavoured with paprika and garlic, are usually sautéed with *vino* (wine), but can also be grilled or stewed.

3. Mariscos
Mariscos, or seafood, is a prominent part of Spanish cuisine, with many dishes featuring *berberechos* (cockles), *almejas* (clams), *mejillones* (mussels) and *pulpo* (octopus).

4. Aceitunas
The Arabic name for olives, *aceitunas* are available in many varieties – small or large, green or black, salty or sweet, whole or stuffed.

5. Champiñones al Ajillo
A popular Spanish tapas dish featuring mushrooms sautéed with garlic, olive oil and lemon juice.

6. Jamón Serrano
Jamón serrano or cured ham is often served as a complimentary slice over a *copa* (glass) as a *tapa* (lid) or as part of a *tabla serrana* (plate of cured meat and cheese).

7. Albóndigas
Albóndigas, or meatballs, are made from either meat or fish, usually stewed in tomato sauce with garlic and spices.

8. Anchoas and Boquerones
Anchoas (cured anchovies) are typically batter-fried, while fresh anchovies, known as *boquerones*, are marinated in oil or served with tomato sauce.

9. Croquetas
This delicious dish is made from deep-fried patties of meat, fish or vegetables mixed with mashed potatoes and béchamel sauce.

10. Alioli
A garlic mayonnaise that can be paired with various dishes.

BODEGAS AND WINERIES

1 Bodegas Fundador

B5 C/Puerta de Rota s/n, Jerez de la Frontera Hours vary, check website bodegasfundador.site

Founded in 1730, this legendary bodega is known for its sherry. A visit to its famous Moorish-style cellar, "de la Ina", is a must when in Jerez.

2 González-Byass

B5 C/Manuel María González 12, Jerez de la Frontera Hours vary, check website Mon tiopepe.com

Although most of the main sherry producers are now largely owned by British multinationals, encouragingly, this bodega was bought back by its original family members. Founded in 1835, González-Byass has two historic cellars, as well as its original tasting room, which remains intact.

3 Bodegas Osborne

B5 C/Los Moros, El Puerto de Santa María, Cádiz osborne.es

The black bull seen on Andalucían roadside hills is the symbol of this venerable sherry and brandy maker and a part of regional heritage.

4 Sandeman

B5 C/Pizarro 10, Jerez de la Frontera Hours vary, check website sandeman.com

Founded in London in 1790, Sandeman created one of the first trademark images in 1928 – the distinctive silhouetted figure of The Don, cloaked in a black cape and wide-brimmed hat.

5 Bodegas Alvear

D3 Avda de María Auxiliadora 1, Montilla Hours vary, check website alvear.es

Alvear is known for its distinct aromatic wines, which are aged in traditional *tinajas* (giant terracotta containers) that give the wines their unique character. Their vessels are carefully buried underground to keep their contents at a constant temperature, while the hot climate ripens the grapes for a stronger wine.

6 Bodegas Málaga Virgen

D4 A-92 km 132, Finca Vistahermosa Fuente de Piedra, Málaga bodegasmalagavirgen.com

Producing traditional Málaga wines of the finest quality, this historic bodega has remained in the hands of the same family for four generations.

Stacked wine barrels at Bodegas Barbadillo

7 Bodegas Barbadillo

B5 C/Sevilla 6, Sanlúcar de Barrameda 11am–3pm Tue–Sat (by appt) barbadillo.com

A family-owned winery with 5 sq km (2 sq miles) of vineyards, Barbadillo has the largest cellars in Sanlúcar. Since launching its first manzanilla in 1827, the winery has grown to house a winemaking museum. Today, it produces a range of wines, including one of Spain's top white wines.

8 Bodegas Andrade

B4 Avda de la Coronación 35, Bollullos Par del Condado, Huelva bodegasandrade.es

Andrade was one of the first bodegas to realize the potential of the Zalema grape for creating young wines.

9 Bodegas Robles

D3 Ctra N331 Córdoba-Málaga km 47, Montilla bodegas robles.com

This organic wine producer ages wines using the traditional *solera* system, in which young wines are blended with older ones, until they mature.

10 Bodegas Góngora

C3 C/Stmo Cristo de la Vera Cruz 59 Hours vary, check website bodegasgongora.com

Located in the Aljarafe region of Seville, this beautiful *bodega* has over 350 years of wine making experience.

Wine tasting hall at Bodegas Osborne

TOP 10 SHERRIES AND WINES

1. Fino
A clear, crisp and dry sherry with an almond aroma, best served chilled as an aperitif.

2. Manzanilla
A dry and slightly salty *fino* sherry, made in Sanlúcar de Barrameda.

3. Oloroso
An amber-coloured sherry with a hazelnut aroma, produced through oxidative ageing.

4. Amontillado
Amontillado falls between a *fino* and an *oloroso* as its layer of flor yeast is allowed to die off, leading to a darker colour.

5. Palo Cortado
This sherry has an aroma reminiscent of an *amontillado*, while its colour is closer to *oloroso*.

6. Raigal
This is one of Andalucía's few sparkling wines, known for its refreshing taste.

7. Pedro Ximénez
This naturally sweet wine, when aged with care, is elegant and velvety.

8. Brandy de Jerez
Produced exclusively in Jerez, this brandy is made by ageing wine spirits in casks previously used for sherry.

9. Málaga
Málaga's famous sweet wines are made from the Moscatel and Pedro Ximénez grape varieties.

10. Cream Sherry
A popular international sherry made from *oloroso* and sweetened with Pedro Ximénez wine.

Glasses of wine and sherry

ANDALUCÍA FOR FREE

1 Patios, Córdoba

D3

Since Roman and Moorish times, Córdoba's inner courtyards have been used to gather, relax and escape the summer heat. Many of the oldest are in the Alcázar Viejo district, between the Alcázar and San Basilio. There are more such spots in Santa Marina, and near la Magdalena, and in Judería. Guides take groups on tours but you may explore those open to the public for yourself. Every May, Córdoba celebrates the 12-day Fiesta of the Patios – an event included on UNESCO's Intangible Cultural Heritage list – when locals decorate their courtyards and open them to the public.

2 Archivo General de Indias, Seville

This UNESCO-listed building *(p92)* was commissioned by Philip II in 1573 as a merchant's exchange and designed by architect Juan de Herrera. The archive contains more than 80 million documents, including letters sent by Columbus to his royal patrons, Fernando II and Isabel I.

3 Cathedral, Seville

Explore this magnificent 15th-century cathedral *(p26)*, set on the rectangular base of an Almohad mosque. Choral masses are held at 8:30am daily from October to May.

4 El Mirador de San Nicolás, Granada

Wander up to this high plaza *(p125)* to enjoy a panoramic view of the Alhambra and surrounding districts and, on clear days, the peaks of the Sierra Nevada. It's a short walk up the hill from Plaza Nueva *(p65)* through the winding cobblestone alleys of the Albaicín area. There are hop-on, hop-off buses for those with limited mobility.

5 Torre del Oro, Seville

This 12-sided military watchtower built by the Almohad dynasty in the 13th century was used to control access to Seville via the Guadalquivir river and later became a prison *(p89)*. Its golden sheen comes from its building materials – mortar, lime and pressed hay – reflected in the river. Note, visitors can explore the tower for free on Mondays.

6 Street Art, Granada

Far removed from the ancient artistic wonders of the Alhambra, Granada's side streets and broad walls serve as rough canvases for talented street artists and their bold and modern graffiti. Some works are inspired by abstract Expressionist painter José Guerrero, while many pieces are witty and at times controversial.

Colourful blooms in a patio, Córdoba

7 Alcazaba and Gibralfaro Castle, Málaga

E5 C/Gibralfaro 11, Distrito Centro 9am–8pm daily (Nov–Mar: to 6pm) alcazabamalaga.com

This Moorish fortress offers the chance to explore Málaga's heritage and architecture. Admission is free every Sunday from 2pm.

8 Fundación Picasso Casa Natal, Málaga

U4 Plaza de la Merced 15 9am–8pm daily fundacionpicasso.malaga.eu

The birthplace of Picasso, now a museum showcasing his artworks, is free to visit on Sunday between 4pm and 8pm.

9 Ruinas de Acinipo, near Ronda

D5 Ctra Ronda-Sevilla km 22 951 04 14 52

Founded in 45 BCE to house retired soldiers from the Roman legions, the Acinipo ruins include a Roman theatre that is still in use today.

10 El Torcal de Antequera

Known for its striking limestone rock formations, El Torcal offers excellent hiking terrain *(p112)*. It features three marked trails, with trek durations ranging from 30 minutes to three hours.

Hiking the cliffs at El Torcal de Antequera

TOP 10 BUDGET TIPS

1. In both the city and province of Granada, tapas are usually served free with drinks in most bars. However, in some bars in the provinces of Almería and Jaén, a small charge may apply.

2. For lunch, try the *menú del día* (daily special), which is reasonably priced and typically includes two or three courses.

3. If you're out for drinks, ordering the house wine or beer on tap is more budget-friendly.

4. When booking trains, choose affordable options with operators such as Iryo *(iryo.eu)* or Renfe *(renfe.com)*. Renfe offers free passes and discounts applicable to various age groups and group travel.

5. Buy a tourist pass or *bono turístico* – the Granada Card, Málaga Card and Sevilla Card cover public transport and offer discounted or free entry to attractions. Note, discount *bonos* are available in Jaén, Úbeda, Baeza and Ronda.

6. To enjoy Marbella on a budget, explore the old town, where prices are more reasonable.

7. Visitors from outside the EU who are departing with purchased goods valued at €90.15 or more are eligible for a refund on Spain's 21 per cent sales tax (VAT, locally known as IVA).

8. Experience free flamenco performances by street performers and buskers in Seville at Plaza de España, Puerta Jerez and the Alameda areas. Many bars and clubs also host flamenco nights.

9. Avoid travelling to major cities during *Semana Santa* (Easter Week), as accommodation rates can significantly increase. August can also be an expensive month for visitors.

10. Consider camping, especially if you're walking in Grazalema, the Alpujarra or Sierra Nevada. Campsites are at high altitudes and are relatively cool and pleasant, even in summer. Prices begin at €5 per tent per night.

RELIGIOUS FESTIVALS

1 Fiesta de los Reyes Magos

5 Jan

Traditionally, this festive evening commemorates the arrival of the Three Kings at the infant Jesus's manger crib. Parades across the region feature the trio, lavishly dressed, progressing through towns in small carriages drawn by tractors or horses. The next day, Epiphany, is when children receive gifts.

2 Carnaval

Feb

Most Andalucían towns celebrate this Catholic festival *(p35)*, but the most spectacular extravaganza is held in Cádiz. Costumes and masked balls are the order of the day and night during these chaotic revels. The implicit anarchy encourages all types of political satire – one of the reasons Franco attempted to abolish the event.

3 Semana Santa

Easter week

Holy Week is observed in every town and village in the region, with dramatic and spectacular processions, especially in Seville *(p88)*. Effigies of Christ and the Virgin are carried through the streets on huge floats. Dressed in traditional outfits, people either maintain penitential silence or express commiseration with the suffering Lord and His mournful Mother.

4 Fiesta de las Cruces

3 May

The Festival of the Crosses celebrates the discovery of the 4th-century True Cross by St Helena. Modes of veneration vary widely in the region, but may include competitions for creating the most beautifully decorated flower-decked cross.

5 Corpus Christi

May/Jun

This festival celebrates the miracle of Transubstantiation, when the Host becomes the body of Christ and the wine, his blood. Granada's celebration is the most famous, with parades and partying, followed by bullfights and flamenco.

6 Romerías

May–Oct

The term *romería* originates from the ancient pilgrimages once made by devotees to Rome. Today, nearly every community hosts its own *romería,* which usually begins with a

Statue of the Virgin on a boat, Virgen del Carmen

colourful pilgrimage to a shrine outside the town, followed by several days of festive celebration.

7 San Juan

23 & 24 Jun

This feast, in celebration of John the Baptist, is popular in many parts of Andalucía. In many communities, the day is marked with midsummer fireworks and bonfires.

8 Virgen del Carmen

15 & 16 Jul

Many coastal communities honour the Virgin Mary, the patron saint of sailors, with a feast. During the event, statues of the Virgin are placed on a flower adorned fishing boat and carried out to sea.

9 Assumption of the Virgin

15 Aug

At the height of summer, the Virgin Mary's assumption into heaven is celebrated, marking the start of the Feria de Málaga, a week-long party. It also commemorates the city's reconquest by the Catholic Monarchs in 1487.

10 Fiesta de San Miguel

Last week Sep–first week Oct

This mix of bullfights, exhibitions and dancing is particularly noteworthy in Seville, Úbeda and the Albaicín quarter of Granada. In Torremolinos, it closes the summer season in festive style.

Enjoying a performance during Carnaval, Cádiz

TOP 10 FERIAS AND OTHER FESTIVALS

1. Flamenco Festivals
Summer months
Throughout the region, these festivals spotlight both traditional and contemporary flamenco dance.

2. Moros y Cristianos
Throughout the year
This festival commemorates historical conquests, with re-enactments of Christian takeovers of local towns.

3. Feria de Abril
Apr/May
Held in Seville two weeks after Easter, this is Spain's largest fair *(p90)*.

4. Wine Festivals
Apr–Sep
Celebrations of the fruit of the vine take place with *La Vendimia* (grape harvest).

5. Feria del Caballo
May
This fair in Jerez de la Frontera centres on Andalucían horses.

6. Music and Dance Festivals
Jun & Jul
Granada hosts many such festivals, such as Spicemas, a carnival celebration that features parades and various competitions.

7. Feria de Jamón
15 Aug
This festival celebrates ham cutting and hosts various activities, including scavenger hunts.

8. Sherry Festivals
Sep–Oct
The towns of the "Sherry Triangle" *(p111)*, notably Jerez, celebrate their fortified wines during harvest season.

9. Fiesta de la Aceituna
1st week Dec
The olive harvest is celebrated in Martos, a town in Jaén Province.

10. Fiesta de los Verdiales
28 Dec
Held at Puerta de la Torre in Málaga Province, this festival, dating back to Moorish times, is a day for playful pranks and wearing amusing hats.

AREA BY AREA

La Giralda, the bell tower of Seville's cathedral

SEVILLE

Andalucía's capital city, Seville combines aristocratic grandeur with a relaxed atmosphere. It has always been tied to the Río Guadalquivir ("the great river" in Arabic), which has been vital to the city's trade and growth. Today, much of its riverfront is made up of an attractive tree-lined promenade, while its historic centre has a wealth of culture, art and architecture, plus plenty of charming neighbourhoods. Most of the key attractions – such as its cathedral, Moorish and Renaissance palaces, and fine museums – are within walking distance of one another.

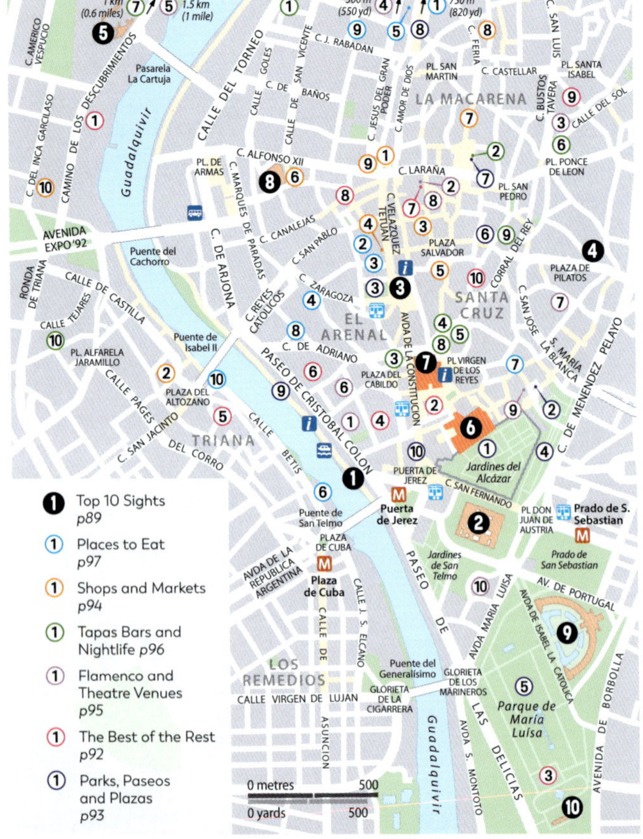

For places to stay in this area, see p146

Torre del Oro overlooking the Río Guadalquivir

1 Torre del Oro

L4 Paseo de Colón 954 22 24 19 9:30am–7pm daily (from 10:30am Sat, Sun & public hols)

The imposing 13th-century dodecahedral (12-sided) watchtower, the Torre del Oro (Tower of Gold) was originally built as part of the city's defences. The *oro* (gold) in the tower's name may refer to the gilded tiles that once adorned its walls or it may have been derived from the tower's initial use as a warehouse for the gold that came in from the Americas during Seville's heyday. Today, it houses a small maritime museum. Nearby stands the Torre del Plata (Tower of Silver), also built to defend the city.

2 Real Fábrica de Tabacos

M5 C/San Fernando 4 954 55 11 23 8am–8:30pm Mon–Fri

A part of Seville University, this stately 18th-century edifice is the second-largest building in Spain. Famous for its fun-loving workers, who at one time rolled three-quarters of Europe's cigars, the old factory has been immortalized by *Carmen*, the most popular opera in the world. The doomed heroine, a hot-blooded *cigarrera*, remains, for many, a symbol of Spanish passion. For guided tours, call ahead to book.

3 Ayuntamiento

L3 Plaza Nueva 1 955 47 02 64 7pm & 8pm Mon–Thu, to 10am Sat

This building has been the town hall since the 16th century. Inside, the rooms are decorated with historic paraphernalia of the city and the monarchy, in a blend of Gothic and Renaissance styles. Outside, the façades reflect the evolution of taste, from the original Renaissance Plateresque work with its finely carved stonework on the eastern side to the 19th-century attempt to copy the style on the west. In front of the building is Plaza Nueva, which hosts regular outdoor markets.

4 La Casa de Pilatos

N3 Plaza de Pilatos 1 9am–6pm daily (Apr–Oct: to 7pm) fundacionmedinaceli.org

Erroneously said to be based on the house of Pontius Pilate in Jerusalem, this 15th-century gem is the most splendid of Seville's urban mansions. It blends Mudéjar, Gothic and Renaissance styles, punctuated with Classical statuary and *azulejo* (Spanish painted ceramic tile) designs. Look for the carved head of the Antinous, the Greek boy who drowned and was deified by his lover, Emperor Hadrian. Medinaceli family portraits are also on display. Note, the upper floor can only be accessed through guided tours, which can be booked online.

5 Monasterio de la Cartuja de Santa María de las Cuevas

J1 C/Américo Vespucio 2 Centro Andaluz de Arte Contemporáneo: 11am–9pm Tue–Sat, 10am–3:30pm Sun caac.es

This 15th-century monastery has had ups and downs over the centuries. During Spain's age of prosperity, it was the favoured retreat of Christopher Columbus, whose remains were interred here for several decades. The monks here decorated their vast enclave with commissions from some of Seville's greatest artists – most of which are now in the Museo de Bellas Artes. In 1841, the monastery became a ceramics factory. Finally, the complex came to house an art museum, the Centro Andaluz de Arte Contemporáneo.

6 Real Alcázar

This lavish palace *(p28)* was mainly the brainchild of Pedro I, who had it built as a luxurious love-nest for himself and his mistress, María de Padilla.

7 Seville Cathedral

Legend has it that when the *Sevillanos* decided to build their cathedral *(p26)* in the 15th century, they wanted to make it so huge that posterity would call it outrageous. As a result, they built the largest church (by volume) in Christendom, along with a mighty Moorish bell tower, La Giralda.

8 Museo de Bellas Artes

K2 Plaza del Museo 9 955 54 29 42 Aug: 9am–3pm Tue–Sat; Sep–Jul: 9am–9pm Tue–Sat, 9am–3pm Sun

This museum, second only to the Prado in Madrid, houses a range of great Spanish paintings. The collection is on display in a former 17th-century convent and focuses on the Seville School, led by Cano, Zurbarán, Valdés Leal and Murillo. Look out for Murillo's touching *Virgen de la Servilleta*. Don't miss El Greco's poignant portrait of his son and the polychrome terracotta

FERIA DE ABRIL

The seven-day Spring Fair, celebrated two weeks after Easter, is a spectacle of colour and high spirits. Horses strut on parade, ridden by *caballeros* in traditional leather chaps, waistcoats and wide-brimmed *sombreros cordobeses*, often with women in flamenco attire perched behind. The air is alive with music, the fairgrounds overflow with *casetas* (party tents – mostly by invitation only), and partying continues until dawn. All festivities take place south of the river.

Paintings on display at the Museo de Bellas Artes

of St Jerome by Florentine sculptor Pietro Torregiano, who was a colleague of Michelangelo.

9 Plaza de España
N6

This semicircular plaza was designed as the centrepiece for the Ibero-American Exposition of 1929. Almost completely covered with gorgeous glazed tiles, its surfaces depict historic moments and heraldic symbols of the 40 regions of Spain. A canal follows the arc of the structure, crossed by colourful footbridges. The site was used as a set in the film *Star Wars: Attack of the Clones* for its otherworldly feel.

10 Museo Arqueológico
N6 Plaza de America
955 12 06 32 For renovation until 2027

This Renaissance-style pavilion, designed by architect Anibal González, was also one of the fabulous structures created for the 1929 Exposition and now houses Andalucía's principal archaeological museum. The assemblage of artifacts ranges from Palaeolithic finds, exhibited in the basement, to splendours of Roman and Moorish art displayed upstairs. The Carambolo treasures of Tartessian gold, also on display in the basement, and the Roman sculpture collection are outstanding.

La Giralda towering above the city

A WALK AROUND THE BARRIO DE SANTA CRUZ

Morning

Start at the exit to the **Real Alcázar** *(p28)* on Patio de las Banderas. Turn right into the **Arco de la Judería**, a covered alleyway that leads to the **Callejón del Agua**, along the old Jewish Quarter's southern wall. Peek into some of the lush patios of these perfectly whitewashed houses – the writer Washington Irving once stayed at No 2. After the wall ends, find the **Jardines de Murillo** *(p93)* on your right, and enjoy a tranquil stroll.

Turn back to **Plaza Santa Cruz** *(p93)*, where the church that gave the neighbourhood its name once stood. A 17th-century wrought-iron cross stands here now. Cross a few streets west to find the **Hospital de los Venerables**. Take in its delightful central courtyard and art gallery.

For lunch, try traditional tapas at the old **Casa Plácido** *(p97)*.

Afternoon

After lunch, head east to **Calle Santa Teresa 8**, the former home of the great artist Bartolomé Esteban Murillo *(p58)*, who died here in 1682.

Finally, walk to the **cathedral** *(p26)* along Calle Mesón del Moro and then to **Calle Mateos Gago**. At No 1 you'll find the **Cervecería Giralda** *(954 22 82 50)*, excellent for a drink or food at any time of day.

Beautiful mosaics in the Casa de la Condesa de Lebrija

The Best of the Rest

1. Pabellón de la Navegación

J1–J2 Camino de los Descubrimientos 2 Hours vary, check website pabellondelanavegacion.com

This museum traces the history of maritime exploration and Seville's rich nautical heritage.

2. Archivo General de Indias

M4 Avda de la Constitución 3 954 50 05 28 9:30am–5pm Tue–Sat, 10am–2pm Sun & public hols

Home to a vast collection of documents, this archive offers insight into the Spanish colonization of the Americas.

3. Museo de Artes y Costumbres Populares

N6 Plaza de América 3 955 54 29 51 9am–9pm Tue–Sat (mid-Jun–mid-Sep: to 3pm), 9am–3pm Sun

Exhibits at this museum include displays on flamenco and traditional bullfighting.

4. Hospital de la Caridad

L4 C/Temprado 3 Hours vary, check website santa-caridad.es

A hospital founded by reformed rake Miguel de Mañara. Its chapel contains artworks by Sevillian artists.

5. Barrio de Triana

K4

Barrio de Triana was once known for producing bullfighters, flamenco artists and fine ceramics.

6. Real Maestranza

L3 Paseo de Cristóbal Colón 12 9:30am–9:30pm daily (Apr–Oct: to 9pm) visitaplazadetorosdesevilla.com

The so-called "Cathedral of Bullfighting" becomes the focal point of Seville when the sporting season begins in April.

7. Casa de la Condesa de Lebrija

M2 C/Cuna 8 10am–6pm daily (Jul–Aug: Mon–Sat) palaciodelebrija.com

A 15th-century Sevillian mansion adorned with intricate mosaics from Itálica *(p101)*.

8. Museo de las Ilusiones

M1 C/ San Eloy 28 10am–7pm daily (to 10pm Fri & Sat) moisevilla.es

An infinity room, an anti-gravity room and a vortex tunnel are some of the highlights at this museum of illusions.

9. La Macarena

N1

Famous for the Semana Santa *(p84)*, this district is home to the Rococo Iglesia de San Luis, the Convento de Santa Paula and the Virgen de la Macarena.

10. Museo del Baile Flamenco

M3 C/Manuel Rojas Marcos 3 11am–6pm daily museodelbaileflamenco.com

Run by famous dancer Cristina Hoyos, this museum explores the wonderful world of flamenco dancing.

Parks, Paseos and Plazas

1. Real Alcázar

Surrounding the oldest palace in Europe, these gardens *(p28)* are a blend of Moorish and Italian Renaissance styles.

2. Plaza Santa Cruz

N4

Built after Napoleon's soldiers destroyed a church that once stood here, this square is now marked by an iron cross known as La Cruz de la Cerrajería.

3. Plaza de San Francisco

L3

Seville's oldest square, Plaza de San Francisco (also known as Plaza Mayor or main square) hosts many public events. Nearby, Plaza Nueva offers a pleasant park featuring a monument dedicated to Fernando III the Saint.

4. Jardines de Murillo

N4

These formal gardens were once the orchards and vegetable plots for the Alcázar. Donated to the city in 1911, they are named after Seville painter Bartolomé Esteban Murillo *(p58)*. Highlights include the Columbus monument which features the bronze prows of the *Santa María*, the caravel that bore the explorer to the Americas in 1492.

5. Parque de María Luísa

M6

This huge park dominates the southern end of the city. Its present design, comprising the Plaza de España, was laid out for the 1929 Exposition. Keep an eye out for peacocks in the trees.

6. Plaza de la Alfalfa

M2

Once the location of the hay market, and later a Sunday morning pet market, the Alfalfa is now a perfect spot for browsing. It is home to many clothing stores, flamenco boutiques, unique accessory shops and bars.

7. Plaza de la Encarnación

M2

This plaza has been completely pedestrianized and now features shops, bars, an observation deck, a market and a subterranean museum. It is dominated by the Metropol Parasol, a huge wooden structure that looks like a cluster of giant mushrooms, hence its nickname, *Las Setas*.

8. Alameda de Hércules

M1

Set off by pairs of columns at either end – the southern set are ancient Roman – this popular promenade is lined with trendy bars and restaurants, which draw a hip crowd.

9. Paseo Alcalde Marqués de Contadero

L4

With the Torre del Oro *(p89)* at one end, this walkway runs along the left bank of the Río Guadalquivir. Inaugurated in 1979, it makes for a pleasant riverfront stroll.

10. Avenida de la Constitución

M5

This pedestrian promenade, which converges with Calle San Fernando, runs through the heart of Seville and is livened up by art exhibitions.

Metropol Parasol in the Plaza de la Encarnación

Shops and Markets

Entrance to the popular Ceramica Triana

1. El Corte Inglés

L2 Plaza del Duque de la Victoria 8 954 59 70 00

Although you're unlikely to find any bargains here, the range of merchandise is impressive. Spain's main department store chain carries not only clothes and accessories, but also perfumes, housewares and sporting goods. There's also a gourmet food section and a food hall, as well as a supermarket.

2. Ceramica Triana

J4 C/Callao 14 954 33 21 79

Home of the famous Triana pottery, this shop sells everything from replicas of 16th-century tiles to ashtrays. The old ceramics factory next door is now a museum.

3. La Guarnicioneria Lopez

M3 C/Cuna 34 954 21 69 23

For quality handmade leather goods, from wallets and handbags to equestrian gear and fashionable accessories, this is the place to go.

4. Massimo Dutti

L2 C/Velázquez 12

massimodutti.com

Tucked along a street lined with chic boutiques, this iconic Spanish chain is known for its fashionable and timeless designs.

5. Aurora Gaviño

M3 C/Álvarez Quintero 16

628 24 56 26

This is a good spot to splurge on all the flouncy dresses, mantillas, shawls and so forth that are needed to participate in the various festivals that abound in the region.

6. Art Market

K2 Plaza del Museo 9

9am–2pm Sun

Shop for unique and original souvenirs from Seville at this market, where local artists display their works.

7. Botellas y Latas

M1 C/Regina 14 954 29 31 22

This wine merchant and delicatessen offers a large selection of excellent Spanish wines and gourmet regional produce. Carlos, the owner of this establishment, is very welcoming.

8. Mercadillo El Jueves

M1 C/Feria 43 8am–3pm Thu

Located just off the Alameda de Hércules *(p93)*, the eclectic Mercadillo El Jueves flea market is Seville's most famous second-hand market. It consists mostly of old junk, books and posters. Nonetheless, it's a fun spot to look for the occasional treasure.

9. Hippy Market

L2 Plaza del Duque de la Victoria

9am–8:30pm Wed–Sat

Find handmade jewellery, leather goods, clothes and other hand crafted items at this lively street market.

10. Torre Sevilla Shopping Centre

J2 C/Gonzalo Jiménez de Quesada 2 cctorresevilla.com

Enjoy endless shopping and a range of delicious food while taking a pleasant walk in the lovely outdoors at this open-air shopping centre in the heart of Seville.

Flamenco and Theatre Venues

1. Teatro de la Maestranza

L4 Paseo de Cristobal Colón 22
teatrodela-maestranza.es

Built as part of Expo '92, Seville's main theatre serves primarily as the city's opera house, with productions of all the classics, particularly those set in Seville, including *Carmen*, *Don Juan* and *The Barber of Seville*.

2. Casa de la Memoria de al-Andalus

M2 C/Cuna 6 Hours vary, check website casadelamemoria.es

Dedicated to flamenco, this cultural centre hosts exhibitions, concerts and dance performances.

3. Sala Cero

N2 C/Sol 5
salacero.com

This venue, known for its beautiful interiors, showcases regional music and theatre productions.

4. Teatro Alameda

L1 C/Crédito 11
teatroalamedasevilla.org

Contemporary Andalucían drama and flamenco feature strongly at this popular, modest theatre.

5. Teatro Central

J1 C/José de Gálvez 6, Isla de Cartuja 955 92 91 29
Jul–Sep

In season, this theatre hosts the *Flamenco Viene del Sur* series, with theatre, dance and classical music.

6. Tablao El Arenal

L4 C/Rodo 7 tablaoelarenal.com

This venue has hosted flamenco performances for more than four decades. Visitors can enjoy tapas, drinks or a full meal while watching the performers. Pay for the first show and enjoy the second one free.

7. La Carbonería

N3 C/Céspedes 21A
954 22 99 45

This relaxed flamenco bar features live performances on Monday and Thursday.

8. Teatro Flamenco Sevilla

M2 C/Cuna 15 5:30pm, 7:30pm & 9pm daily teatroflamencosevilla.com

A unique venue where acclaimed artists bring alive the emotions of flamenco, with dance and music.

9. Los Gallos

N4 Plaza de Santa Cruz 11
7pm & 8:45pm daily tablaolosgallos.com

Watch excellent flamenco artists – many of whom are winners of national and international awards – impress at the oldest *tablao* in Seville.

10. Teatro Lope de Vega

M5 Avda de María Luísa
teatrolopedevega.org

This Neo-Baroque theatre, named after the "Spanish Shakespeare", was built in 1929 as a casino and theatre for the Ibero American Exposition. Both modern and classical works are performed here.

Ornate hall of the Teatro Lope de Vega

Enjoying a drink at El Rinconcillo

Tapas Bars and Nightlife

1. Sala Malandar
K1 C/Torneo 43
salamalandar.com
Come to this-laid back club for an eclectic array of music – from funk to reggae and ska via soul, folk and indie pop – performed by live bands and DJs.

2. Premier Sherry Cocktail Bar
L3 C/San Pablo 9
955 13 30 32
This vibrant bar offers an excellent selection of wine, sherry and cocktails. Tastings are available for groups.

3. Casa Morales
L3 C/García de Vinuesa 11
954 22 12 42
Opened in 1850, this bar is reputedly the second-oldest in the area. Drinks are still poured from traditional casks and served alongside simple tapas.

4. Antigüedades
M3 C/Argote de Molina 40
954 56 51 27
The eccentric decor of this bar, which changes regularly, features Roman and Arab elements. Traditional cuisine and reasonably priced drinks attract locals and tourists alike.

5. Pura Vida Terraza
M3 Hotel Los Seises Sevilla, C/ Segovias 6 667 71 74 44
Chill out, sip a cocktail and enjoy stunning views of the city at this lively rooftop pool and bar.

6. El Rinconcillo
M2 C/Gerona 40 954 22 31 83
The city's oldest *taberna* dates from 1670 and is an essential stop on your Seville itinerary. It offers an excellent selection of Moorish-Andalucían food.

7. Antique Theatro
C/Matemáticos Rey Pastor y Castro, La Cartuja 666 55 05 50 Mon–Wed
Dress to impress at Seville's most upscale club, and you might just get past the doormen. In summer, the rooftop club Rosso hosts live events.

8. La Terraza del EME
M3 C/Alemanes 27, 4th floor of EME Catedral Hotel laterrazadeleme.com
Enjoy spectacular views of the cathedral and La Giralda while sipping a cocktail on the terrace bar of the upmarket EME hotel.

9. Bar El Garlochi
M2 C/Boteros 26
A Seville institution with religious decor, known for its Baroque exuberance and lively locals. Try *Sangre de Cristo,* their signature cocktail.

10. Puratasca
J3 C/Numancia 5
puratasca.com
Discover delicious twists on the classics at this fusion tapas bar, where the menu changes with the seasons.

Places to Eat

1. Restaurante Arte y Sabor
M1 Alameda de Hércules 85
695 28 84 50 · €

A selection of Moroccan and Spanish cuisine, with options for vegans and vegetarians, is offered at this restaurant. The terrace is a great place to sit back and enjoy the Alameda vibe.

2. Lobo López
L3 C/De Rosario 15
854 70 58 34 · €

Tucked away on a side street, this smart restaurant offers a fusion of international cuisine. Try the scallop risotto with shrimp tartare.

3. Casa La Viuda
L3 C/Albareda 2
954 21 54 20 · €

Choose from a wide variety of classic dishes and tapas at this Michelin-starred Sevillian bodega. Don't miss their famous cod.

4. Taberna del Alabardero
L3 C/Zaragoza 20
alabarderosevilla.es · €€

Excellent meat dishes and local seafood form the heart of the menu at this taberna set in a lavish mansion.

5. El Disparate
M1 Alameda de Hércules 31
somoseldisparate.com · €€

Expect fresh Mediterranean cuisine made using local and seasonal ingredients at this innovative Michelin-starred restaurant.

6. Abades Triana
L5 C/Betis 69
abadestriana.com · €€€

This modern restaurant has a commanding location on the river. Diners can book a spot in El Cubo, a private area with a "floating" glass floor. There are tapas and gourmet tasting menus on offer.

PRICE CATEGORIES

For a three-course meal for one with half a bottle of wine (or equivalent meal), taxes and extra charges

€ under €30 €€ €30–€50 €€€ over €50

7. Casa Plácido
M3 C/Mesón del Moro 11
casaplacido.es · €

Hams dangling, barrels of sherry, old posters and traditional tapas are on offer at this venerable bar.

8. Mechela Arenal
L3 C/Pastor y Landero 20
mechela.es · €€

Mechela Arenal has a modern approach to traditional recipes using fresh, local ingredients. Try the white prawn carpaccio with avocado pesto.

9. Espacio Eslava
L1 C/Eslava 3–5
espacioeslava.com · €€

This tapas bar and restaurant adds a dash of innovation to traditional cuisine using fresh, seasonal produce.

10. Mariatrifulca
K4 Puente de Isabel II
mariatrifulca.com · €€

Enjoy a contemporary twist to classic Sevillian food while admiring stunning views of the city and the Guadalquivir. Prime cuts of meat are also on offer.

Outdoor seating at the Casa La Viuda

SEVILLA AND HUELVA PROVINCES

Leaving behind the magnetic allure of glorious Seville, the rest of Sevilla Province and neighbouring Huelva Province are among the least visited areas of Andalucía. Much of the region has retained its rural charm, where time seems to move at a slower pace and the traditional customs still thrive. This area is also home to some of the finest nature reserves, including Parque Nacional de Doñana, along with rugged mountains and pristine beaches. These quieter areas are generally favoured by locals rather than tourists, and make a refreshing change from the crowds typically found in other parts of Andalucía. The cities here offer an abundance of pretty plazas, historical monuments and, as you might expect being so close to a bustling port, a wealth of seafood bars and restaurants.

For places to stay in this area, see p147

Horses grazing in the picturesque town of El Rocío

1 El Rocío

B4

This town's resemblance to an Old West frontier outpost is no accident. The Spaniards who are now settled in the states of Texas, New Mexico and Arizona – parts of the popular Wild West – mostly came from this region and took the architectural style with them. Horseback is still a common mode of transport here. The town comes alive during its annual *romería* *(p84)*.

2 Parque Nacional de Doñana

Europe's largest nature reserve *(p42)* has wetlands and shifting dunes that are gradually moving inland. Most fragile areas can only be visited on guided tours.

3 Huelva

A4

Founded by the Phoenicians, Huelva peaked under Roman rule and later prospered during the early days of trade with the Americas. The city is also famous as the launching point of Columbus's voyage to the New World, an event marked in the Museo de Huelva (*museosdeandalucia.es*), which also has exhibitions charting Ríotinto's history. Admission is free for EU citizens.

4 El Parque Minero de Ríotinto

B3

A detour off the N435 between Huelva and the Sierra de Aracena leads to the opencast mines at Ríotinto (Red River). Considered the oldest in the world, these mines have been worked for over 5,000 years. Centuries of extraction have created a moonscape-like terrain with colourful fissures. This area is also home to the fascinating Museo Minero (*parquemineroderiotinto.es*), which traces its long mining history.

5 Carmona

C3

The closest major town east of Seville, Carmona has been inhabited for over 5,000 years. Its Roman remains are exceptional, with its huge necropolis *(Avda Jorge Bonsor 9)* standing out as a highlight. The town features many fine churches, palaces and *alcázares* – one of its ancient castles is now a spectacular parador. It is also home to the Roman Puerta de Córdoba (Córdoba Gate), which offers sweeping views of the plains.

6 Cazalla de la Sierra

C3

This main town in the Sierra Norte is a steep cluster of whitewashed houses. It's a popular place for weekend get-aways by *sevillanos* and particularly known for producing some of the area's famous anise-based tipples. Just 3 km (2 miles) away lies La Cartuja de Cazalla *(lacartujadecazalla.com)*, a former Carthusian monastery, which has been restored as a part hotel and part wellness centre. It's also an excellent spot for astrotourism.

7 Écija

D3

Two nicknames for this town east of Seville give an idea of its chief glory and its biggest challenge. "The Town of Towers" refers to its 11 Baroque bell towers, all adorned with glazed tiles. "The Frying Pan of Andalucía" alludes to its searing summer temperatures, which rise high due to the fact that it's one of the few towns not on a hill. The town's Museo Histórico Municipal *(museo.ecija.es)* focuses on its history and archaeology through a rich collection of Roman artifacts.

8 Gruta de las Maravillas

B3 C/Pozo de la Nieve, Aracena 10am–2pm & 3:30–6pm daily aracena.es

A guided tour of these marvellous caves winds through beautiful chambers with naturally coloured formations and names such as the Hut, Organ, Cathedral, Quail and Twins. The last room – *Sala de los*

SOCIALISM VERSUS FEUDALISM

The fertile Campiña valley in Sevilla has been owned by noble families since the Catholic Monarchs handed out fiefdoms. The workers were little more than serfs. Now, however, the mayor of Marinaleda, a town in the region has created an island of social idealism – wresting property away from individuals to be communally owned by the workers.

Bell tower overlooking the town of Carmona

Culos (Chamber of the Buttocks) – is a notorious crowd-pleaser. There are 12 caverns and six underground lakes. The "Great Lake" lies under a vaulted ceiling, 70 m (230 ft) high.

9 Itálica

B3

These windblown ruins were once part of the third-largest city in the Roman Empire. Founded in 206 BCE, Itálica was home to half a million people during the reign of Emperor Hadrian in the 2nd century CE. Both Hadrian and his predecessor Trajan, another native of the city, transformed the city with marble temples and grand buildings. At the heart of the complex are the remains of an amphitheatre and some mosaics amid the crumbling walls. Much of the site still lies buried, and many of its treasures have been moved to the Museo Arqueológico *(p91)* in Seville. Note, entry is free for EU citizens.

10 Osuna

D4

The city of Osuna was once a major hub of Renaissance Spain, which has resulted in some exceptional architectural gems such as the church, the Colegiata and the University. It is also known for its fine mansions, most notably the Palacio del Marqués de la Gomera *(p50)*, a testament to Baroque splendour. The Museo de Osuna *(turismodeosuna.es)* houses a number of important artworks, as well as a permanent exhibition featuring costumes and memorabilia from the popular TV series *Game of Thrones*, which was filmed here.

Exhibit in the Museo de Osuna

A DAY IN SANTIPONCE

Morning

Venture 7 km (4 miles) north of Seville to Santiponce, a town famous for the ruins of the Roman city Itálica. Make your way to the **Monastery of San Isidoro del Campo** *(Avda de San Isidoro del Campo 18)*, founded in 1301 by Alonso Pérez de Guzmán. This vast complex has two churches, and is a juxtaposition of Gothic, Baroque, Languedoc and Mudéjar design.

From the monastery, it's a 20-minute walk north to the **Cotidiana Vitae** *(Plaza de la Constitución)*, close to the **Teatro Romano de Itálica** *(open only for concerts or plays)*. This cultural centre re-creates the daily life of the Romans of the 2nd century CE.

Leaving the centre, head north on Avenida de Extremadura and turn right on Avda Rocio Vega to reach **La Caseta De Antonio** *(Avenida Rocío Vega 10; 955 99 63 06)* for a delicious lunch.

Afternoon

After lunch, head to **Itálica**, the first Roman city on the Iberian Peninsula. Stroll through the grounds of the ancient settlement, passing some astonishing mosaics, a temple, the remains of thermal baths and the 2,500-seat **amphitheatre**.

Round off the afternoon with a cup of coffee from your pick of the Spanish restaurants near the ruins.

The Best of the Rest

1. Jabugo

B3

Spain's most famous hams, including *jamón ibérico* (cured Iberian ham), *jamón serrano* (mountain-cured ham) and *pata negra*, named after the black pigs that forage in the Sierra de Aracena, are made in Jabugo, a town often called the "home of ham".

2. Niebla

B4

Massive ramparts, built by the Moors in the 12th century, attest to the central role this town played in defending the land. The walls stretch for about 2.5 km (1.5 miles).

3. Sierra de Aracena y Picos de Aroche Park

B2

Hiking is a popular activity in this park, thanks to its stunning landscapes and rich flora and fauna. Many trails run through its protected natural areas and the local villages.

4. Aroche

A2

This well-preserved village contains a wonderful oddity, the Museo del Santo Rosario *(859 99 30 38; hours vary, call ahead)*, packed with rosaries that have belonged to Mother Teresa, John F Kennedy and General Franco.

5. Cortegana

B3

One of the largest towns in the area, Cortegana is dominated by a 13th-century castle.

6. Aracena

B3

A lovely historic town, Aracena sits at the foot of a ruined Moorish fortress perched on a hillside.

7. Almonaster la Real

B3

This village's most notable landmark is its well-preserved 10th-century mosque located within a castle.

8. Santa Olalla del Cala

B3

Nestled in the heart of the ham-curing region, this village has a 13th-century castle and a 15th-century Baroque church.

9. Alájar

B3

A charming town featuring cobbled streets and whitewashed buildings.

10. Zufre

B3

This cliff-top town is like a mini-Ronda. Its promenade, the Paseo de los Alcaldes, offers sweeping views across the plain.

Moorish fortress overlooking the town of Aracena

Shopping

Leather boots for sale at Valverde del Camino

1. Aroche Markets

Thursday is the day the market stalls arrive in this Huelvan town. The market in Plaza de Abastos features a traditional produce spread, including the strong-flavoured goat's cheese favoured by the locals.

2. Souvenirs

In Aracena, head for the Calle Pozo de la Nieve, a cobbled street lined with souvenir shops. In El Rocío *(p99)*, souvenir stalls flank the church, hawking objects associated with the *romería* pilgrimage *(p84)*.

3. Crafts

In addition to leather, Valverde del Camino is known for furniture and fine wooden boxes. Embroidery work from Aracena and Bollullos del Condado is worth seeking out, as are linen tablecloths from Cortegana and Moguer. Wickerwork is widely sold around Huelva, while nearer the coast it is also common to see Moroccan goods for sale.

4. Anise Liqueur

The liqueur of choice throughout the region is anise-based. One of the best is Anis Cazalla, from the eponymous town of Cazalla de la Sierra *(p100)*.

5. Ham

The Mesón Sánchez Romero Carvajal in Jabugo is one of the top producers of the local *jamón ibérico*.

6. Cured Fish

Considered a great delicacy and priced accordingly, *mojama* (raw wind-cured tuna) is an acquired taste. Isla Cristina is the main centre of production, but you can also buy it in the Mercado del Carmen in Huelva, and other food markets.

7. Leather

The most notable leather goods come from Valverde del Camino. Choose between *botos camperos* (cowboy boots) and the longer *botos rocieros* (Spanish riding boots). Many shops produce footwear, and a number of crafters make boots to order, taking three to four days to make a pair. There are workshops devoted to making saddles and bridles, too.

8. El Condado Wine District

The name refers to an area famous for its refreshing white wine. Local *finos* include Condado Pálido and Condado Viejo.

9. Huelva

The provincial capital *(p99)* has its own El Corte Inglés department store on Plaza de España, while the area around it and just off Plaza 12 de Octobre constitutes the main shopping district. The Mercadillo (open-air market) is held every Friday on the Recinto Colombino.

10. Pottery

In this area, the pottery has traditional patterns influenced by Moorish art. Look for water jugs, plates and jars, decorated in blue, green and white glazes.

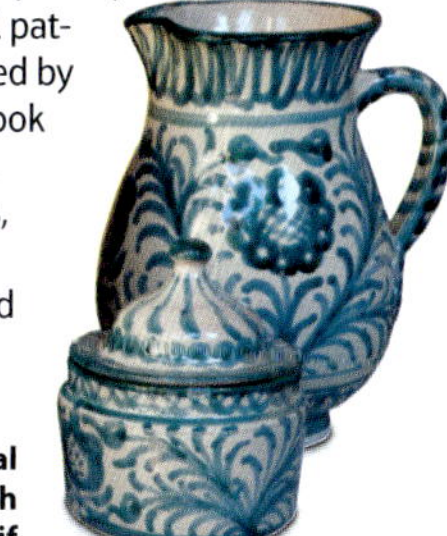

Traditional pottery jar with a floral motif

Cafés and Tapas Bars

Narrow street with mixed façades in historic Carmona

1. Taberna Alota Muelle 3 Carabelas, Huelva

A4 Muelle 3 Carabelas
664 44 46 43 Mon

Savour traditional food at this delightful family-friendly spot, conveniently located near replicas of Christopher Columbus's ships.

2. Bar Goya, Carmona

C3 C/Prim 2 Wed
goyatapas.com

This café bar is set in a 15th-century, Moorish-style building in the heart of Carmona. Its speciality includes Andalucían home cooking with a modern twist.

3. El Martinete, Cazalla

C3 Ctra Estación de Cazalla km 12 687 49 39 65 Mon–Wed

Enjoy good-value tapas and seasonal, local produce in a beautiful setting surrounded by woods and waterfalls.

4. Bar La Reja, Écija

D3 C/Cintería 16 954 83 30 12
Sun & Mon

A local favourite, this spot offers a wide choice of tapas and *raciones* in a relaxed atmosphere that invites you to linger.

5. La Puerta Ancha, Ayamonte

A4 Plaza de la Laguna 14
Sun lapuertaancha.es

A sociable place that purports to be the original town bar, La Puerta Ancha serves reasonably priced tapas, drinks and other snacks. Savour them alfresco on tables set on the square.

6. Chiringuito Bombadill, Isla Canela

A4 Paseo de Los Gavilanes s/n
Tue bombadill.es

Set right on the beach, this charming restaurant specializes in fresh fish and delicious rice dishes. Enjoy stunning sunsets from the terrace as you dine.

7. El Refugio, Mazagón

B4 C/Santa Clara 43
624 52 69 79 Tue

A laid-back, popular haunt located a short stroll from Playa de Mazagón *(p68)*, El Refugio is a family-owned business renowned for its fresh fish dishes.

8. Bar Cafeteria La Reja, Aracena

B3 Ctra N433 km 87
959 12 76 70

This tapas bar specializes in regional food, including wild mushrooms, local cheeses and snails.

9. Nuevo Manzano, Aracena

B3 Plaza del Marqués de Aracena 22 687 42 91 24
D Tue & Wed

On the south side of the town square is this traditional bar perfect for coffee and a pastry.

10. Casa Curro, Osuna

D4 Plazuela Salitre 5
955 82 07 58 Mon

Just a few blocks from the main square, this premier tapas bar offers an elaborate menu in a cosy neighbourhood setting. It's the ideal spot to enjoy traditional Spanish fare.

Places to Eat

1. La Choza de Manuela, Bormujos

B4 C/Menendez Pidal 2
chozademanuela.com · €

Popular with locals, this restaurant specializes in a variety of succulent, grilled meats, served by friendly staff. Go early to avoid the long queues.

2. Meson Rey Arturo, Osuna

D4 C/Sor Angela 3 662 13 22 21
Sun–Tue & D Sat · €€

Feast on creative interpretations of regional and international cuisine, such as *croquetas de chipirones en su tinta con alioli de higo* (squid croquettes in their ink with fig *alioli*).

3. Restaurante Miramar, Punta Umbría

A4 C/Miramar 1 959 31 12 43 · €

An unpretentious beach bar, this restaurant serves fresh fish from the Atlantic, usually paired with rice dishes.

4. Restaurante Montecruz, Aracena

D3 Plaza de San Pedro 36
959 12 60 13 · €€

Expect exceptional food at this restaurant, where local, organic produce is key, featuring game, ham, chestnuts and wild mushrooms when in season.

5. Cambio de Tercio, Constantina

C3 C/Virgen del Robledo 53 bajo, Constantina 955 88 10 80
Tue & D Sun–Thu · €

This place is popular with fans of rural cookery. Specialities include Iberian pork loin in wild mushroom sauce, and for dessert, *tarta de castañas* (chestnut tart).

6. Restaurante Azabache, Huelva

A4 C/Vázquez López 22
959 25 75 28 D Sat & Sun · €€€

A smart traditional restaurant popular with locals and known for its *raciones*, or large servings of *tapas*.

PRICE CATEGORIES

For a three-course meal for one with half a bottle of wine (or equivalent meal), taxes and extra charges.

€ under €30 **€€** €30–€50 **€€€** over €50

7. Casa Luciano, Ayamonte

A4 C/Palma del Condado 1
Sun casa-luciano.es · €€

This is the place for fresh, tempting seafood and fish stews. Try the delicious *coquinas* (steamed baby clams) or the appetizing grilled calamari.

8. Aires de Doñana, El Rocío

B4 Avda La Canaliega 1 Mon
airesdedonana.com · €€

Enjoy panoramic views of the marshes while feasting on goose liver pâté, beef burger and blueberry cheesecake.

9. Posada de Cortegana, Cortegana

A2 Ctra El Repilado – La Corte km 2.5 posadadecortegana.es · €€

A wide variety of meat, such as Iberian pork, venison and game, is on offer at this lovely grillhouse.

10. Casa El Padrino, Alájar

B3 Plaza Miguel Moya 2 959 12 56 01 Mon–Thu · €

This rustic favourite is known for its tasty regional dishes, especially its Padrino pork shoulder.

Thatched *choza* dwellings in Doñana National Park, Huelva

MÁLAGA AND CÁDIZ PROVINCES

These two Andalucían provinces offer sights in abundance and a wealth of culture and leisure. Europe's oldest city, Cádiz, is found here, where rich history meets hedonistic pleasures and stunning beaches. Here, too, are the region's most dramatic landscapes, inevitably popular with nature lovers, and Andalucía's famous *pueblos blancos* (white villages), with Ronda – the birthplace of one of Spain's oldest traditions, the bullfight – the most renowned. This area is also home to the world-famous fortified wine known as Jerez (sherry), and the celebrated sweet wines of Málaga. Finally, Tarifa, mainland Europe's southernmost point and something of an alternative enclave, offers stunning views of North Africa, with the Rock of Gibraltar just a stone's throw away.

For places to stay in this area, see p147

Puente Nuevo linking the two sides of Ronda

1 Ronda

To many visitors, Ronda *(p36)* evokes the "real" Andalucía, wild and spectacular. This mountain rock eyrie is breathtaking, being dramatically sliced down the middle by El Tajo, a fantastically deep and narrow limestone ravine, formed over thousands of years by the Río Guadalevín. The Puente Nuevo bridge spans this impressive gorge, making Ronda a town of two halves – the ancient half is steeped in rich Moorish history, with cobbled streets, while the more modern part is on the north side.

2 Cádiz

At the apex of the Atlantic's untamed Costa de la Luz *(p111)*, ancient Cádiz *(p34)* floats on what was originally its own island. It is possibly Europe's oldest city, thought to have been founded by the Phoenicians in around 1104 BCE. Much of what can be seen today, however, dates from the 18th century – the city was destroyed by an Anglo-Dutch raid in 1596. The Catedral Nueva (1722), one of Spain's largest churches, and many Baroque edifices grace this unpretentiously beautiful provincial capital. Apart from two weeks in February when Cádiz stages Spain's most celebrated Carnaval *(p35)*, it remains under-visited.

Mediterranean Sea

1 Top 10 Sights p107

1 Costa del Sol Places to Eat p115

1 Places to Eat across the Region p117

1 Costa del Sol Nightlife p114

1 Nightlife across the Region p116

1 The Best of the Rest p112

3 Málaga

E5

Despite being home to the main airport bringing holidaymakers to the Costa del Sol, this provincial capital has been bypassed by the brunt of "sun coast" development and has managed to hold onto its Spanishness quite admirably. It has a thriving arts scene and attracts foodies to its many restaurants. Its modern waterfront complex has bars, shops, the Centre Pompidou Málaga *(p57)*, as well as a lively promenade and space for plush yachts. Important as a trading port since ancient times, it was the favourite city of poet Federico García Lorca *(p58)*, who loved its rawness. But its even greater claim to artistic fame is that it was the birthplace of Pablo Picasso, whose creative genius is celebrated in the Museo Picasso *(p56)*. Málaga's alcázar, built between the 8th and 11th centuries, includes a Roman amphitheatre.

4 Antequera

D4 turismo.antequera.es

So ancient that even the Romans called it Antiquaria, this market town presents a wonderfully condensed architectural history of the entire area, beginning with Neolithic dolmens dating from between 4500 and 2500 BCE. In addition, there are significant Roman ruins, including villas with outstanding mosaics, a Moorish Alcazaba *(p53)*, the 16th-century Arco de los Gigantes and fine Renaissance palaces and churches to explore. Many treasures originally found in the town – including the exquisite Ephebe of Antequera, a rare, life-size Roman bronze statue of a young boy – are displayed in the Museo Municipal *(p57)*, housed in an 18th-century palace.

5 Gibraltar

C6

This gargantuan chunk of limestone rising up from the Mediterranean was one of the mythic Pillars of Hercules. Yet, despite being nicknamed "The Rock", as a worldwide symbol of stability and security, this fortress is the subject of contention between Spain and Great Britain. Nonetheless, many people cross the border to visit this slice of England today. The town centre is home to museums, restaurants and shops, and from here visitors can take a cable car to the Upper Rock. Here, several interesting attractions can be found, including St Michael's Cave, the tunnels from the Great

Mijas, one of Andalucía's popular *pueblos blancos*

Siege of 1779–83 and tunnels from World War II. The Skywalk lookout, perched at 340 m (1,115 ft) above sea level, and the Windsor Suspension Bridge offer incredible views. Don't miss the Apes' Den, which houses one of Gibraltar's most iconic residents: the Barbary macaques (tailless monkeys).

6 Pueblos Blancos

C5

The term "white villages" refers to the profusion of whitewashed hillside hamlets in the Serranía de Ronda, the mountainous territory around Ronda. Many are truly beautiful and it's well worth spending several days driving from one to the other, and then setting out on foot to take in some of the views. Towns not to miss include Gaucín, Mijas, Casares, Grazalema *(p112)*, Setenil, Zahara de la Sierra *(p60)*, Jimena de Libár and Manilva. Villagers, who originally settled here to protect themselves from bandits in the lowlands, retain a centuries-old way of life and strong agricultural tradition. Between Grazalema and Zahara, you'll go through Andalucía's highest mountain pass, the breathtaking Puerto de las Palomas (The Pass of the Doves).

Distinctive Rock of Gibraltar rising from the sea

A MORNING WALK IN JEREZ DE LA FRONTERA

Begin at the impressive **Alcázar**, with its many Moorish remains, including restored gardens, a mosque, a hammam (baths) and a *camera obscura* providing magnificent views. Beside it is the stunningly decorated **cathedral**, extravagantly rich inside and out. Admire *The Sleeping Girl* by Zurbarán in the sacristy.

Next, take the tour – with tastings – of the **González-Byass** *(p80)* bodega, one of the oldest cellars in Jerez. Don't miss the many signatures of famous people on the barrels (called "butts"), including Queen Victoria, Cole Porter, Martin Luther King and General Franco.

Continuing on north, the Moorish **Bodegas Fundador** *(p80)* also offers tours. A block further north, pass the Gothic-style Church of San Mateo, then pop into the **Museo Arqueológico** to see the prized Greek bronze helmet from the 7th century BCE, and then enter the **Barrio de Santiago**. This gently dilapidated neighbourhood of maze-like alleyways is home to a sizable Roma community and numerous flamenco venues.

To cap off your walk, continue southeast out of the *barrio*, past the **Church of San Dionisio**, then turn back to **Tabanco Plateros** *(C/Algarve 35; 956 10 44 58)*, for some light tapas and a great selection of wine and cheese.

Postcard-worthy Calahonda Beach in Nerja, Costa del Sol

7 The Costa del Sol

This string of former Mediterranean fishing villages *(p38)* still lives up to its reputation as one of the world centres for sun, surf and fun. But beyond the bustling tourist enclaves there is still much authentic charm on offer and even places that invite tranquillity – especially in the towns of Estepona, Nerja, Mijas and the ultra-classy Marbella *(p67)*. Year-round golf makes the whole area a great attraction for international fans of the sport and, in high season in particular, Torremolinos *(p67)* is the place to find some of Spain's liveliest nightlife.

8 Jerez de la Frontera

B5 Alcázar de Jerez: C/Alameda Vieja Plaza del Arenal, Edificio Los Arcos; turismojerez.com

The largest city in Cádiz Province, Jerez is synonymous with sherry – a word derived from Jerez, which in turn came from the Phoenician Xeres. Long before that, the city was part of the Tartessian civilization dating back to the 8th century BCE. Today, visitors can explore its Moorish fortress, Alcázar de Jerez de la Frontera, once part of a 4-km (2.5-mile) defensive wall. Within the complex is a well-preserved mosque, now the chapel of Santa María La Real. The city is also known for its equestrian art and flamenco tradition *(p54)*.

9 Arcos de la Frontera

C5 C/Cuesta de Belén 5; 956 70 22 64

Another town built atop a sheer cliff, Arcos de la Frontera is probably the most dazzling of the *pueblos blancos* and the one situated furthest west. Little remains of the period before the *Reconquista*, when it received its "de la Frontera" appellation, as a bastion "on the frontier" between Christian and Moorish Spain. The town is also home to the Galería de Arte Arx-Arcis *(C/Marqués de Torresoto 11)* crafts museum and shop, which displays local carpets, blankets, baskets and pottery.

10 The Costa de la Luz

B5–C6

Named for the shimmering sunlight it receives *(luz)*, this stretch of coast from Huelva down to Tarifa is the opposite of the Costa del Sol. Its largely untouched coastline is peppered with stunning beaches and charming Andalucían towns. The low-key resorts attract mainly Spanish visitors and water-sports lovers – the latter drawn by the strong ocean breezes. But here, you will also find beaches backed by shady pine forests, and the combination of Arabic forts, Moorish castles, medieval churches, sherry and old-school charm makes the Costa de la Luz a great choice for adventurous holidaymakers.

THE SHERRY TRIANGLE

Jerez, Sanlúcar de Barrameda and El Puerto de Santa María mark the famed "Sherry Triangle". Production of the fortified wine was started by the Phoenicians using vines they imported some 3,000 years ago. In Roman times it was exported all over the empire, and it has been popular in England since the Elizabethan Age. Sherry varies in degrees of dryness or sweetness. The *fino* and *manzanilla* are dry and light, while the *amontillado* and *oloroso* are more robust *(p81)*.

Whitewashed buildings at Arcos de la Frontera

Walkway stretching across the El Chorro

The Best of the Rest

1. El Torcal de Antequera

D4

This mountain nature reserve is great for hiking. The odd limestone rock formations are a big draw.

2. El Chorro

D4

A geographical wonder, the Chorro Gorge's immense chasm, 180 m (590 ft) high, was created by the Río Guadalorce slashing through the limestone mountain. A 7.7-km- (4.7-mile-) long path, El Caminito del Rey, runs along the gorge.

3. Grazalema

C5

Nestled in the foothills of the Sierra del Pinar, Grazalema is a charming village – Spain's rainiest, according to some – and the main access point for the Sierra de Grazalema Natural Park *(p67)*, one of the best hiking areas in Andalucía. Known for its local cheeses, stews and honey, it's also a great place for a picnic.

4. Tarifa

One of Andalucía's hippest coastal towns, Tarifa *(p116)* features a sizable windsurfing and kitesurfing *(p70)* contingent. You'll also find various Moroccan touches here.

5. Algeciras

C6

Although this town is industrial and polluted, its port is the best in Spain; from here you can catch the ferry to Morocco. Peruse the Moorish bazaars while waiting for the boat.

6. El Puerto de Santa María

B5

One of the Sherry Triangle towns, several bodegas can be visited here for tours and tastings.

7. Sanlúcar de Barrameda

B5

Famed for its *manzanilla* sherry and superb seafood, the town also has beautiful churches and palaces and also offers tours of its bodegas.

8. Chipiona

B5

This pretty resort town is crowded with Spanish beach enthusiasts in high season. The pace of life here is leisurely, consisting of enjoying the surf and miles of golden sand during the day, then strolls and ice cream in the evening.

9. Vejer de la Frontera

C6

Of all the *pueblos blancos* *(p109)*, this one has kept its Moorish roots most intact. Its original four Moorish gates still stand and its streets have barely changed in 1,000 years.

10. Iglesia de Santa María la Coronada, Medina Sidonia

C5 Plaza Iglesia Mayor
956 41 03 29 Hours vary, call ahead

The most important edifice in Medina Sidonia is the 15th-century church of Santa María la Coronada, built over an earlier mosque. Its interior features a 15-m- (50-ft-) high *retablo*.

Shopping

1. Málaga Wines

T5

This region is famed for its sweet wines, and Málaga has plenty of establishments where they can be sampled and purchased. El Templo del Vino *(C/de Sebastián Souvirón 11)* is particularly well stocked with local tipples and also with wines from all over Spain.

2. Chocolates Artesanales Frigiliana

E5 C/Real 27, Frigiliana
669 20 90 56

Set in a picturesque village, Chocolates Artesanales Frigiliana sells over 15 unique chocolate flavours and a range of cosmetics, all made with a natural chocolate base.

3. Deligades, Cádiz

B5 C/Libertad 9 956 21 35 21

This gourmet shop sells an array of wine, cheese, ham, olive oil, sweets and other delicacies of the region.

4. Sasha Alpargatas, Cádiz

B5 C/Sacromonte 24
sashalpargatas.es

The place to go for stylish espadrilles, Sasha Alpargatas has everything, from suede, leather and canvas to other natural fabrics.

5. Flamenco Costumes

B5

Jerez *(p110)* is one of the very best places to find genuine flamenco gear. Tamara Flamenco *(tamara flamenco.com)* offers a wide range of flamenco accessories.

6. Equestrian Equipment

B5

La Casa del Campo Tienda Hípica *(tiendahipicalcdc.es)* in Jerez is the ideal place to shop for equestrian gear, while Hipisur *(hipisur.com)* offers an extensive selection of clothing and equipment.

7. Sherry

Jerez de la Frontera *(p110)* is, of course, also the prime spot to savour the finer points of a *fino*, a *manzanilla*, an *amontillado* or an *oloroso*. Visitors can buy sherry and also join a tasting tour at Bodegas Fundador *(p80)*.

8. Traditional Textiles

Grazalema and Arcos de la Frontera *(p110)* are known for their blankets, ponchos, rugs and other woven textiles. At Mantas de Grazalema *(mantasdegrazalema.com)* you can tour the factory and purchase excellent traditional souvenirs.

9. Shopping in Gibraltar

The shopping draw here *(p108)* is twofold: there's no sales tax and it's mostly duty-free. Several UK high-street names are represented, such as Next and Marks & Spencer.

10. Leather

For some of the best prices on leather goods in Spain, visit Miscelánea *(miscel anea.online)*, which offers a wide range of leather goods, from handbags to shoes.

Bottles of sweet dry wine from Málaga

Costa del Sol Nightlife

1. Ocean Club, Marbella

D5 Avda Lola Flores
oceanclub.es

A chic club featuring a saltwater swimming pool and a VIP area with huge round beds.

2. La Suite, Marbella

D5 Puente Romano Hotel, Bulevar Príncipe Alfonso von Hohenlohe
952 89 09 00 Sun–Wed

Live it up at this club with fire-eaters, belly dancers and jugglers. In the summer, the club becomes Suite del Mar and moves beachside.

3. Club de Jazz y Cócteles Speakeasy, Fuengirola

D5 Pasaje de las Rampas
656 48 79 19

Styled after the speakeasies of the 1920s, this bar has live jazz music at weekends and great cocktails.

4. Mango, Benalmádena

D5 Plaza Solymar 952 56 27 00

Popular with the younger crowds, this club has an electric atmosphere.

Dinner with a view at Ocean Club, Marbella

5. Olivia Valère, Marbella

D5 Ctra de Istán km 0.8
olivia-valere.com

This exclusive club is a Costa hot spot. Designed by the same creative genius who did Paris's famous Buddha Bar, it attracts a well-heeled crowd.

6. Puerto Marina, Benalmádena

D5 Puerto Marina

A large complex located in the heart of Benalmádena, Puerto Marina has a variety of bars, nightclubs, shops and restaurants.

7. El Mico Bar, Torremolinos

E5 Edificio Delphine, C/Jaén 2, Local 13 711 01 17 15

Karaoke, quiz nights, drag shows and live entertainment draw large crowds at this bar.

8. Gran Madrid Casino Torrequebrada, Benalmádena

D5 Avda del Sol casinotorrequebrada.com

Located in the Hotel Torrequebrada, this casino has tables for blackjack, chemin de fer, punto y banco and roulette. Note, the casino has a smart dress code.

9. La Taberna de Pepe Lopez, Torremolinos

E5 Plaza de la Gamba Alegre
952 38 12 84 Sun

This flamenco venue is highly touristy, but fun. Shows take place here between 10pm and midnight.

10. Torremolinos for LGBTQ+ Nightlife

E5

Torremolinos has the best LGBTQ+ nightlife on the Costa del Sol. Start at the terrace bar El Gato *(Paseo Marítimo Antonio Machado 1)*, then try Parthenon *(C/ Nogalera)* before heading to Centuryon *(C/ Casablanca 15)*, the biggest LGBTQ+ club outside Madrid or Barcelona.

Costa del Sol Places to Eat

Alfresco dining at the sea-themed Bar Altamirano

PRICE CATEGORIES

For a three-course meal for one with half a bottle of wine (or equivalent meal), taxes and extra charges.

€ under €30 **€€** €30–€50 **€€€** over €50

1. La Pappardella, Marbella

D5 Muelle de Honor, Casa A, local 4, Puerto Banús 952 81 50 89 · €€€

Enjoy Neapolitan cuisine at this family-friendly restaurant with a wide range of pasta, pizza and seafood.

2. El Canarias, Plaza del Remo, Torremolinos

E5 Plaza del Remo s/n elcanariasplaya.com · €€

Savour traditional specialities like *espetos* (sardines grilled on skewers), fried fish and seafood rice dishes here.

3. El Estrecho, Marbella

D5 C/San Lázaro 12 609 40 93 36 Sun & Mon · €

A local favourite, this tapas bar serves seafood, *fino* and *boquerones al limón* (anchovies in lemon).

4. La Sirena, Benalmádena

D5 Paseo Maritimo Mon lasirenarestaurante.es · €€

Located on the beachfront, La Sirena offers one of the best *paellas* in the area.

5. Bodegas Quitapenas, Torremolinos

E5 C/Cuesta del Tajo 3 952 38 62 44 · €

An excellent tapas bar with mouthwatering Spanish seafood, including *pulpo* (octopus).

6. Restaurante La Experiencia, Torremolinos

E5 Avda Joan Miró 19, L6 Entrada 623 43 08 63 Sun & Mon · €€€

An intimate and cosy restaurant, La Experiencia promises an indulgent fine-dining experience. It also has an excellent vegetarian menu.

7. Tapeo de Cervantes, Málaga

E5 C/Cárcer 8 Mon eltapeodecervantes.com · €€

This charming, rustic bodega serves hearty regional food with some novel touches. Try the *estofado de cordero* (lamb stew with mint and couscous).

8. Bar Altamirano, Marbella

D5 Plaza Altamirano 3 952 82 49 32 Mon · €

Despite Marbella's glitzy image, there are still affordable, traditional tapas bars – and this is one of them. Located just southeast of Plaza Naranjos, it features seafood specialities listed on ceramic menus.

9. Restaurante 34, Nerja

E5 C/Hernando de Carabeo 34 Mon hotelcarabeo.com · €€€

Cut into the cliff, this café offers lovely views of the sea while you relax under palm frond umbrellas.

10. Lan Sang, Nerja

E5 C/Malaga 12 952 52 80 53 Sun & L Mon · €€

For a change of cuisine, try this Thai–Laotian restaurant. Its modern, elegant decor is matched by sophisticated flavours and beautiful presentation of the food.

Nightlife across the Region

Flamenco performance at the Peña La Perla in Cádiz

1. Nerja

E5

Plaza Tutti Frutti in Nerja is a great spot to enjoy a night out. Bars and nightspots here offer everything from cocktails to karaoke. The best-known clubs are Seven *(Plaza Tutti Frutti)* and the nearby Sala Rockerfeller *(C/Chaparil 7)*.

2. Málaga

Málaga's *(p108)* vibrant nightlife has something for everyone. The lively Barsovia *(C/Mendez Nuñez 3)* disco attracts people of all ages; students visit ZZ Pub *(C/Tejón y Rodríguez 6)* to hear bands on weekdays. A DJ fills in the quiet moments every night.

3. Marbella

D5

The nightlife in Marbella is lively and diverse thanks to chic beach clubs and bustling town bars. Puerto Banús is the hot spot for a glamorous night, with stylish clubs like Olivia Valere where you can dance until dawn. The old town has numerous tapas bars and cosy taverns perfect for relaxed evening drinks.

4. Ronda

Choose from a variety of bars and clubs, particularly around Plaza Carmen Abela, in Ronda *(p36)*. Café Las Bridas *(C/Virgen de los Remedios 18)* offers imported brews, with live music at weekends from midnight. Dance to Spanish electro-pop at Café Pub Dulcinea *(C/Rios Rosas 3)*.

5. Gibraltar

There are loads of pubs in Gibraltar *(p108)*. For late nights and a great selection of bars, visit Queensway Quay, Marina Bay and Casemates Square.

6. Tarifa

C6

This quaint town transforms at night, offering everything from casual drinks to dancing. Almedina Tarifa *(C/Almedina 3)* is one of the oldest bars, with flamenco on Thursday nights. Nearby, Café del Mar *(Paseo Marítimo)* has three floors and a terrace for sunset views.

7. Cádiz

The harbour in Cádiz *(p34)* is loaded with nightclubs, and Momart Theatre is one of the best. Cádiz also brims with flamenco clubs. Good options include Peña La Perla and Peña Enrique el Mellizo.

8. Sancti Petri

C6

Sip a refreshing cocktail and watch the sunset at one of the popular beach bars along the Costa de la Luz.

9. El Puerto de Santa María

B5

Known for its lively nightlife around the old town and the marina, El Puerto de Santa María has plenty of tapas bars and traditional bodegas serving local sherry, perfect for a relaxed evening. For more energetic nights, clubs like Sala New Palace keep the party going.

10. Jerez de la Frontera

In Jerez *(p110)* you will find flamenco at its impassioned best – the Roma quarter of Santiago is the place to be. Here, you will find a number of *peñas* (clubs), but don't expect much before 10pm.

Places to Eat across the Region

1. Ventorrillo del Chato, Cádiz
B5 Ctra Cádiz-San Fernando km 2 (Via Augusta Julia) 956 25 00 25 • €€€
This is the oldest restaurant in Cádiz (1780) and also one of its best. Try *salmorejo*, a thick tomato soup served as a dip or side dish, and *dorada a la sal*, a local fish baked in a salt crust.

2. Antigua Casa de Guardia, Málaga
T5 Alameda Principal 18 952 21 46 80 D Sun • €
The city's oldest *taberna*, dating from 1840, has barrels of local wine in the bar. Its steamed mussels are great.

3. A Mar Restaurante, Jerez
B5 C/Latorre 8 956 32 29 15 • €€
This small, trendy restaurant serves up quality cuisine, specializing in dishes made with fresh regional seafood.

4. Bar Juanito, Jerez de la Frontera
B5 C/Pescadería Vieja 8 & 10 956 33 48 38 Mon, Tue & D Sun • €
Famous for the best tapas in town, Bar Juanito closes during the Feria in May.

5. Restaurante Los Portales, El Puerto de Santa María
B5 C/Ribera del Marisco 7 956 54 21 16 • €€
Savour traditional Cádiz delicacies in a renovated winery. Fish and seafood are the speciality here.

6. Sollo, Fuengirola
D5 Avda del Higuerón 48 L, Sun & Mon sollo.es • €€€
Chef Diego Gallegos, popularly known as the chef of caviar, creates unusual tapas-style dishes using snail caviar, eels, trout ceviche and ox steak. Treat your taste buds to these gastronomic innovations while feasting your eyes on the superb coastal views.

PRICE CATEGORIES
For a three-course meal for one with half a bottle of wine (or equivalent meal), taxes and extra charges.
€ under €30 €€ €30–€50 €€€ over €50

7. Tragatá, Ronda
D5 C/Nueva 4 952 87 72 09 • €€
Former El Bulli chef Benito Gómez creates the best tapas in Andalucía and stocks local Schatz organic wines.

8. Jardin del Califa, Vejer de la Frontera
C6 Plaza de España 12 califavejer.com • €€€
Exquisite North African and Middle Eastern cuisine is served in an enchanting complex of medieval buildings. Dine in the cool, shaded garden or a stone vaulted cellar.

9. Balandro, Cádiz
B5 Alameda Apodaca 22 restaurantebalandro.com • €€€
Set in an 18th-century mansion overlooking the bay, Balandro serves superb fried and grilled fish.

10. Restaurante Tropicana, Ronda
D5 C/Virgen de los Dolores 11 952 87 89 85 Tue, Wed & D Sun • €€
Expect innovative takes on local and international dishes at this stylish restaurant.

Barrels of local wine in Antigua Casa de Guardia

The grand Catedral Nueva rising above the Campo del Sur promenade, Cádiz

GRANADA AND ALMERÍA PROVINCES

Granada, home to the enchanting Alhambra, the crown jewel of Europe's Moorish palaces, is often admired solely for this iconic monument. Yet beyond its famous cultural treasures, the region is scattered with a diverse array of attractions. Hikers can explore the rugged mountain trails of the nearby Sierra Nevada, while those seeking relaxation will find pristine beaches along the coast. Meanwhile, cinema lovers can visit striking desert locations and original film sets that once brought classic Westerns to life.

Whitewashed houses above Alhama de Granada canyon

1 Catedral, Granada

T2 C/Gran Via de Colón 5
10am–2pm & 3–7pm Mon–Sat
catedraldegranada.com

To establish Christian rule, this triumphalist structure was built by some of the greatest 16th-century architects. The interior of Granada's cathedral is one of its most stunning features, while Alonso Cano's façade echoes the ancient triple arch favoured by Roman emperors. Inside the cathedral complex is the Capilla Real *(capillarealgranada.com)*, one of Granada's finest Christian buildings and a repository of rare treasures, including a *reja* (gilded grille) by

For places to stay in this area, see p148

Bartolomé de Jaén, priceless jewels and paintings by Roger van der Weyden and Sandro Botticelli. Note, it is advisable to book your tickets in advance.

2 Alhama de Granada

E4

Clinging precariously to the edge of a gorge, this whitewashed village was known in Moorish times for its beauty and natural thermal waters (*al-hamma* means "hot spring" in Arabic). The village is home to the Hotel Balneario, which preserves an 11th-century *aljibe* (cistern), graced by Caliphal arches. Nearby is the 16th-century Iglesia de la Encarnación, where some of the vestments on display are said to have been embroidered by Queen Isabel the Catholic.

3 Monasterio de la Cartuja, Granada

F4 Paseo de la Cartuja 958 16 19 32 10am–7pm Mon–Fri & Sun, 10am–12:45pm & 3–6pm Sat

Founded in 1516, this Carthusian monastery has a deceptively austere exterior considering the flamboyant Spanish Baroque detailing that can be found inside its church and sacristy. The busy flourishes and arabesques of polychromed and gilded stucco almost swallow up the architectural lines. The dazzling cupola by Antonio Palomino is a particular highlight.

Splendid interior of the Monasterio de la Cartuja, Granada

4 "Wild West" Towns

G4

The interior of Almería Province resembles the deserts and canyons of the American Southwest: it was the perfect spot for filming the Wild West epics known as "Spaghetti Westerns" of the 1960s and 1970s. Two of the sets are now theme parks: Mini Hollywood *(p75)* and Fort Bravo *(Ctra N340 km 468, Tabernas; fortbravo.org)* offer stunt shows and memorabilia. Here, visitors can re-enact classic film scenes or watch stunt persons performing bank hold-ups or saloon brawls. These sets are occasionally used for TV ads and series.

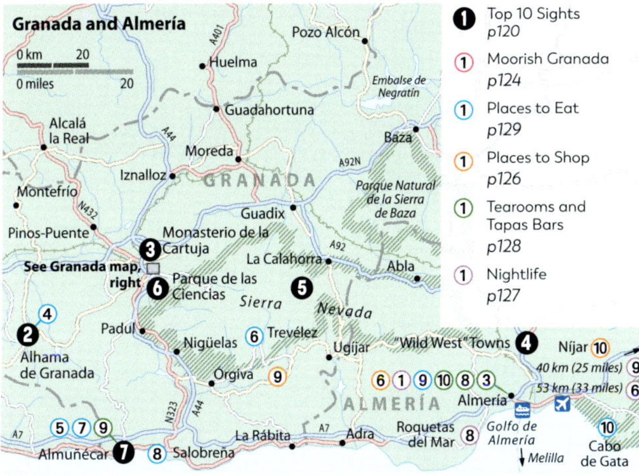

5 Sierra Nevada

Mainland Spain's tallest peaks *(p44)* – and, after the Alps, Europe's second-loftiest chain – make Andalucía perfect for excellent winter sports and robust trekking in spring and summer, as well as abundant wild flowers and wildlife. Stop in the historic villages of the Alpujarras, on the southern slopes, where time seems to have stood still, and see local artisans at work.

6 Parque de las Ciencias

F4 Avda de la Ciencia, Granada 10am–7pm Tue–Sat, 10am–3pm Sun & public hols parqueciencias.com

This exciting complex, dedicated to science and exploration, is made up of numerous interactive areas, such as Journey Through the Human Body, Perception, Eureka and Biosphere. There's an Observation Tower, a Planetarium and the Sala Explora, exclusively for children aged three to seven, where they can conduct their first experiments. There are temporary exhibitions, too.

7 Almuñécar and Around

F5 visitalmunecar.es

The Costa Tropical is a spectacular coast with towering mountains rising from the shore. Almuñécar is the chief town on this stretch and it is almost entirely devoted to resort life. Yet it has an ancient heritage, dating back to the Phoenicians, and was an important port under the Moors. The intriguing archaeological museum here has a unique Egyptian vase dating from the 7th century BCE.

8 Almería and Around

G4

Almería, the "mirror of the sea", has lost much of its shine due to modern development. Still, its 10th-century Alcazaba *(p53)* is one of the most impressive surviving Moorish forts, and there are many spots with North African influences in the old quarter. Note, entry to the Alcazaba is free for EU citizens.

PLASTICULTURA

If you approach the coastal area of these provinces from the west, you will notice the extent of plastic tenting, a phenomenon that reaches its peak before Almería. This agricultural technique is known as *plasticultura* and squeezes out every drop of moisture from these desert lands in order to produce crops. The process has raised environmental concerns and efforts are being made to make the recycling of plastic easier.

Skiing on the snowy slopes of the Sierra Nevada

9 The Alhambra

A visit to the Alhambra *(p22)*, arguably the pinnacle of Europe's Moorish palaces, is a truly special experience. Its magical use of space, light, water and decoration characterizes this most impressive piece of architecture. Built under caliphs Ismail I, Yusuf I and Muhammad V during the Nasrid dynasty, it was meant to depict paradise on Earth. The complex includes the Palacios Nazaríes, 13th-century Alcazaba, 16th-century Palace of Carlos I and the Generalife *(p24)*. Although it suffered pillage and decay, including an attempt by Napoleon's troops to blow it up, it has undergone extensive restoration to preserve its dazzling craftsmanship.

10 Albaicín

U1

This ancient Moorish quarter *(p124)* of Granada clings to the hills opposite the Alhambra, its labyrinth of narrow streets and whitewashed houses evoking centuries of history and culture. Once a fortified suburb, Albaicín's blend of Andalucían and North African architecture charms visitors with traditional teahouses, hidden plazas and striking views over the city and the Sierra Nevada.

A MORNING IN GRANADA

Begin your walk at **Plaza Bib-Rambla**, enhanced with flower stalls and the Neptune fountain. Fronting the western side of the square is the warren of ancient shopping streets called **La Alcaicería** *(p126)*. Don't miss the 14th-century Moorish **Corral del Carbón** and its cultural centre.

When the **cathedral** *(p120)* opens, take a moment to admire the main chapel, a masterpiece by Silóe, and the ornaments and priceless treasures in the Chapter Room. The next stop is the **Capilla Real**; visit the crypt under the ostentatious marble sarcophagi of the kings and queens, where their bodies repose in plain lead boxes. On the carved Renaissance sepulchres, note the split pomegranate, symbol of a defeated Moorish Granada.

Continue on across the busy thoroughfares until you get to the river and the long expanse of **Plaza Nueva** *(p64)*. Choose an outside table at a café (the cafés here are all similar), order a drink and take in the street life.

It's time to enter the labyrinth of the **Albaicín**. Take **Calle Elvira** up to **Calle Calderería Vieja** to explore the vibrant bazaar of the Moorish Quarter. Following the old steep streets, keep going until you reach the fanciful **La Tetería del Bañuelo** *(p128)*, an inviting place to sip some mint tea and sample Moroccan sweets.

Moorish Granada: Albaicín

Medieval pillars and high ceiling of the El Bañuelo

1. El Bañuelo (Baños Árabes)

U2 Carrera del Darro 31 958 57 51 31 Daily

Dating from the 11th century, these are the best preserved Moorish baths in Spain. The rooms were used for changing, meeting, massage and bathing.

2. Real Chancillería

T2 Plaza del Padre Suárez 1 958 02 74 94 8:30am–2pm Mon–Fri

The impressive Royal Chancery, dating from 1530, was built shortly after the *Reconquista* in a futile attempt to Christianize this Moorish quarter. The palace was designed by architect Diego de Siloé.

3. Iglesia de Santa Ana

U2 C/Santa Ana 1 958 22 50 04 11:30am–1:30pm & 6–7:30pm Tue–Sat, 11:30am–2pm & 6:30–7:30pm Sun

At the end of Plaza Nueva stands this 16th-century brick church in Mudéjar style, built by Muslim artisans for Christian patrons. Inside the main chapel is a coffered ceiling in the Moorish tradition. The bell tower was originally a minaret.

4. Iglesia de San Pedro y San Pablo

U2 Carrera del Darro 2 958 22 32 33 10am–2pm Tue–Sat, 10:30am–noon Sun

Across from the Casa de Castril, this church, built in the 1500s, graces an attractive spot on the banks of the river. From here you can see the Alhambra dominating the landscape.

5. Casa de Castril

U2 Carrera del Darro 43 600 14 31 41 Jul–Aug: 9am–3pm Tue–Sun; Sep–Jun: 9am–8pm Tue–Sat, 9am–3pm Sun

This ornate 16th-century mansion was originally owned by the secretary to Fernando II and Isabel I. Since 1879 it has served as the Archaeological and Ethnological Museum, displaying artifacts from Granada's past, from the Palaeolithic era up until the Reconquest in 1492. The remarkable collection is displayed across three galleries and around the central courtyard.

Albaicín with the San Nicolás viewpoint in the centre

6. Tearooms

As you wander around the labyrinth of whitewashed houses and tiny sloping alleyways of the Albaicín quarter you will encounter many tearooms – a Moroccan tradition that is very much alive in this quarter. Possibly the best one, La Tetería del Bañuelo *(p128)*, consists of a series of rooms set amid delightful gardens. Here you can sip your minty brew, nibble on honeyed sweets and contemplate the timeless panorama.

7. Paseo de los Tristes

V2

The broad tree-lined esplanade follows the course of the river upstream. It once accommodated tournaments, processions and funeral cortèges, but now bars and restaurants dominate the scene.

8. Plaza Larga

U1

From the Paseo de los Tristes follow Calle Panaderos to reach this busy market square, where you'll mostly find produce stalls, cheap restaurants and bars. The square sports an Islamic gateway with a typically angled entrance as part of what remains of the upper fortifications. This is the Arco de las Pesas – if you pass through it you will come to the Albaicín's most popular square, Plaza San Nicolás.

Colourful wares for sale in Moroccan shops

9. Moroccan Shops

Check out the hilly streets off Calle Elvira, especially Calderería Vieja and Calderería Nueva, for typically Moroccan shops. The scene is indistinguishable from what you would find in Morocco itself, with the colourful wares spilling out onto the pavements.

10. El Mirador de San Nicolás

U1

In front of the Iglesia de San Nicolás, this magnificent terrace has such lovely views of the Alhambra and the Sierra Nevada that it has long been dubbed El Mirador ("The Lookout Point") de San Nicolás. The views are extraordinary at sunset, when the Alhambra glows softly ochre and the often-snowcapped Sierra Nevada radiates pink in the distance.

Places to Shop

Colourful clothing stalls at a market, La Alcaicería

1. Albaicín, Granada

The rustic Moroccan shops in this ancient quarter *(p125)* are all concentrated on two sloping streets off Calle Elvira – Caldererîa Vieja and Caldererîa Nueva.

2. Cerámica Miguel Muñoz, Granada

T2 Plaza de las Pasiegas 3
675 40 51 20

This traditional ceramics store sells the typical style of the region: blue patterns on white tiles, with a pomegranate motif.

3. Taracea Laguna, Granada

V2 Real de la Alhambra 30
958 22 90 19

Opposite the entrance to the Alhambra, you can see how *taracea* (Moorish marquetry, often inlaid with bone, mother-of-pearl or silver) is made, and take home a souvenir unique to this area.

4. Al Aire Art, Granada

U1 Plaza Aliatar 16 622 36 46 51

Located in the Albaicín area, this small shop features high-quality handmade artworks.

5. El Rocío, Granada

T2 C/Capuchinas 8 958 26 58 23

The complete outfitter for *romería* and festival-going gear. All the frills, polka dots and bright colours will dazzle your eye. They come in every size, so even babies can have a flounce or two.

6. Bazar el Valenciano, Almería

G4 C/Las Tiendas 34
elvalenciano.com

Bazar el Valenciano is the oldest store in town. Look for "El Indalo" souvenirs, which are items bearing the symbol of Almería for good luck.

7. Carrera de la Virgen, Granada

F4

This street has some great gourmet shops. Ibérica *(Carrera de la Virgen 44)*, a deli specializing in local fare, is a must-try, while Abuela Ili *(Carrera de la Virgen 51; abuelailichocolates.com)* is a specialist chocolate shop ideal for those with a sweet tooth.

8. La Alcaicería, Granada

T2

In Moorish times this was the silk market, although the horseshoe arches and stucco are a modern re-creation. The narrow alleyways are bursting with colourful wares such as silver jewellery, embroidered silk shawls and ceramics.

9. Alpujarras Crafts, Granada

F4–G4

The hill towns of this zone are rich in traditional crafts, including ceramics and weaving. Local *jarapas* (rugs), bags, ponchos and blankets are hand-loomed in age-old patterns and sold at local weekly markets.

10. Níjar, Almería

H4

This coastal town is known for its distinctive pottery and *jarapas*. Head to Calle Las Eras, in the Barrio Alfarero, to find genuine articles.

Nightlife

1. La Canastera, Almería

G4 C/Cordoneros 5
662 14 32 31

Enjoy flamenco performances at this venue in the Pescadería neighbourhood of Almería. Shows are held every Thursday and Saturday evening with tickets selling for around €20. Note, only cash is accepted.

2. Sala Vogue, Granada

T1 C/Almona de San Juan de Dios 20 festgra.com/discoteca/sala-vogue

This trendy nightclub in the Realejo district is an indie favourite. It has two rooms, with different vibes and DJs.

3. TragoFino-San Matias 30, Granada

T2 Plaza de las Descalzas 3
665 40 93 12

Popular with locals, this busy bar, located in the heart of Granada, serves a variety of reasonably priced, delicious cocktails. The service is friendly and attentive.

4. Eurostars Gran Vía, Granada

T1 C/Gran Vía de Colón 20
958 21 78 10

Enjoy a cocktail on the terrace with great views of Granada Cathedral and the Alhambra. Indoor and outdoor zones make this a perfect place to visit all year round.

5. Planta Baja, Granada

F4 C/Horno de Abad 11
plantabaja.club

A lively two-storey venue: the upper floor is a quiet bar, while downstairs, the DJs play chart hits. There is live music at the weekends.

6. Abanicos, Almería

G5 C/Goya 2, 04640 Pulpí
abanicosterreros.com

This summer-only bar specializes in cocktails served with a tropical flair.

7. El Camborio, Granada

V1 Camino del Sacromonte 47
Sun & Mon elcamborio.com

This is a popular night venue in the caves of Sacromonte. Music echoes from four dance floors to the rooftop terraces, offering a striking view of the Alhambra at sunrise.

8. Chaplin's Pub, Almería

G5 Calle Sierro 27, Roquetas de Mar 618 82 43 68 Mon–Wed

Watch sporting events, play bar games and enjoy a pint of beer at this classic British pub.

9. Maui Beach, Almería

H4 Paseo del Mediterráneo 40, Mojácar Beach 699 03 03 56

This charming *chiringuito* (beach bar) offers a variety of zones, each with a great ambience. At night, Maui Beach transforms from a bar and restaurant into a lively club.

10. Hanalei Cocktail Bar, Granada

T3 C/Piedra Santa 22
grupoparipe.com/hanalei

Hanalei Cocktail Bar is known for its Tiki cocktails, which are inspired by a fusion of flavours from Polynesia, Brazil and the Caribbean. Served with fiery displays in colourful glasses, these tasty cocktails are a must-try.

Outdoor seating at El Camborio

Tearooms and Tapas Bars

1. La Tetería del Bañuelo, Granada

U2 C/Bañuelo 5 622 47 13 92

The little rooms and intimate niches are suffused with a gentle light, the air with the aromas of tea and flowers and the sound of songbirds. Try sweets and fragrant brews with unsurpassed views.

2. Kasbah, Granada

T2 C/Caldereria Nueva 4

kasbahgranada.com

Relax amid the comforts of this candlelit café. Silky pillows and romantic nooks abound. You can enjoy Arab pastries and a selection of Moroccan teas.

3. Casa Puga, Almería

G4 C/Jovellanos 7 Sun

barcasapuga.es

One of the city's best tapas bars. The wine list is exhaustive, as you might guess from the wine racks on view.

4. Bar La Buena Vida, Granada

T2 C/Almiceros 12 654 63 57 97

A welcoming tapas bar with a good variety of wines and beers. There's free tapas with each drink, so you can sample a wide variety of treats.

5. Casa Enrique, Granada

T3 C/Acero de Darro 8 D Sun

958 25 50 08

Another wonderfully old-fashioned hole-in-the-wall lined with antique barrels. Try the *montaditos de lomo* (small sandwiches with pork fillet) and *torta del casar* (sheep's-milk cheese).

6. Antigua Bodega Castañeda, Granada

T2 C/Elvira 5

casacastaneda.es

Antique wine barrels and hanging hams give this place a rustic feel. The cheese boards are a good bet, as are the *montaditos* (small sandwiches).

7. La Riviera, Granada

T2 C/Cetti Meriem 7

sites.google.com/sesalgado.net/la-riviera

Located in the heart of the city, La Riviera offers a good variety of beer and tapas.

8. Tetería Al Hammam Almeraya, Almería

G4 C/Perea 9 Mon & Tue

almeraya.info

Escape from the crowds in the tranquil tearooms of Almería's Arab baths and enjoy Moorish-inspired teas and snacks.

9. Bodega Francisco, Almuñécar

F5 C/Real 11 958 63 01 68

Ham shanks hanging from the ceiling greet the eye, along with barrels of *fino* in this traditional tapas bar. The attached restaurant, Francisco II, serves full meals.

10. El Quinto Toro, Almería

G4 Juan Leal 6 950 23 91 35

D Mon–Wed, D Sat & Sun

The name derives from the tradition that the best bull of a corrida is chosen to fight in the *quinto* (fifth) confrontation of the day. This bar is a favourite among local bullfight aficionados.

Enjoying a drink at the Casa Puga in Almería

Places to Eat

PRICE CATEGORIES

For a three-course meal for one with half a bottle of wine (or equivalent meal), taxes and extra charges.

€ under €30 €€ €30–€50 €€€ over €50

1. Cunini, Granada

F4 Plaza Pescadería 14
958 25 07 77 D Sun · €€

The fresh seafood, brought in daily from Motril, is highly recommended, and is a big hit with the food critics.

2. Arrayanes, Granada

T2 Cuesta Marañas 4
Tue restaurantearrayanes granada.com · €

An elegant Moroccan restaurant serving tagines, couscous and pastries. Note, all meat is halal and no alcohol is served.

3. Carmen Mirador de Aixa, Granada

U2 Carril de San Agustín 2
carmenmiradordeaixa.com · €€€

Enjoy excellent interpretations of regional dishes such as *habas con jamón* (broad beans with ham) with views of the Alhambra from the terrace.

4. Restaurante El Ventorro, Alhama de Granada

E4 Ctra de Jatar km 2 Mon
elventorro.net · €€

In this lovely rural restaurant you can try Grandma Currilla's potato stew, or savour sumptuous casseroles and grilled meat.

5. Restaurante Mar de Plata, Almuñecar

F5 Avda Mar de Plata 3
restaurantemardeplata.es · €

At this Mediterranean restaurant choose from a wide selection of dishes, particularly focused on fresh fish and seafood. Try the *arroz con bogavante* (rice with lobster).

Beautiful arches in Arrayanes Moroccan restaurant, Granada

6. Restaurante Nuevo González, Trevélez

F4 Plaza Francisco Abellán
restaurantenuevogonzalez.es · €€

This is the perfect spot to try the flavourful ham that the region is known for, while taking in the scenic views.

7. El Chaleco, Almuñécar

F5 Avda Costa del Sol 37
Hours vary, check website
elchaleco.restaurant · €€

French cuisine, lovingly prepared with attention to detail, is served in a romantic, intimate setting.

8. Pesetas, Salobreña

F5 C/Bóveda 11
958 61 01 82 Mon · €

Savour stunning coastal views as you enjoy *choco a la marinera* (squid in tomato sauce). The salads are great, too.

9. Restaurante Valentín, Almería

G4 C/Tenor Iribarne 19 Mon, Sep restaurantevalentin.es · €€

Specialities here include highly delectable *arroz negro* (rice in squid ink) and *pescado en adobo* (marinated fish).

10. La Goleta, San Miguel del Cabo de Gata

H5 Paseo Marítimo Cabo de Gata 950 37 02 15 · €€

All the seafood is at its freshest here since this village is located in the middle of Andalucía's most unspoiled coast.

CÓRDOBA AND JAÉN PROVINCES

These two provinces are an attractive blend of exquisite urban architecture, famed agricultural zones and great wildlife reserves within rugged mountain ranges. The ancient treasure-trove of Córdoba is the star, but the Renaissance towns of Baeza and Úbeda are among the region's most beautiful. For lovers of good food and good wine, the areas around Montilla, Valle de los Pedroches and Baena should not be missed. Meanwhile, nature lovers can hike for days amid the wilds of the Parque Natural de la Sierra de Cardeña y Montoro in Córdoba and the Sierra de Cazorla in Jaén.

1 Córdoba

This town *(p30)*, wonderfully rich in history and cultural importance, is also small enough to cover easily and enjoyably on foot. It has a delightfully contrasting mix of sights, from the architectural splendour of the great mosque – with a Christian church oddly sprouting out of its centre – to the whitewashed glories of the old Jewish quarter, the splendid Alcázar and the Zoco Municipal with its diverse selection of goods made by local artists. There are engaging museums as well, featuring works of art by Old Masters and local artists, and ancient artifacts evoking the area's influential past.

2 Úbeda

Ignore the downtrodden outskirts as you approach this town *(p40)* – once you get to the historic centre you will realize that it is one of Andalucía's most remarkable splendours. The keynote here is architecture – an entire district of Renaissance edifices built for local nobility in the 16th century. One of

For places to stay in this area, see p149

Ruins of the ancient city of Medina Azahara

Andalucía's greatest architects, Andrés de Vandelvira, was the genius who gave most of these structures their harmonious forms.

3 Medina Azahara

D3 Ctra Palma del Río km 5.5, W of Córdoba
Hours vary, check website
museosdeandalucia.es

The building of the first palace here dates from 936 CE, commissioned by Caliph Abd ar-Rahman III, Emir of Córdoba and the man who brought the city to glory. He named it after his favourite wife, Az-Zahra (the Radiant). Though it is little more than a ruin now, at one time it held a zoo, ponds, gardens, baths, houses, barracks, markets, mosques, a harem of 6,000 women and accommodation for 4,000 enslaved people. Night-time visits are possible in the spring and summer months, providing a magical experience. Note, entry is free for EU citizens.

4 Baeza

Like nearby Úbeda, this smaller town *(p40)* is also a jewel of Renaissance glory, but includes earlier remains dating back to the Moors and, before them, the Romans. The town radiates a sense of tranquillity as you walk from one cluster of lovely buildings to another. Again, much of the beauty owes its existence to the architect Andrés de Vandelvira.

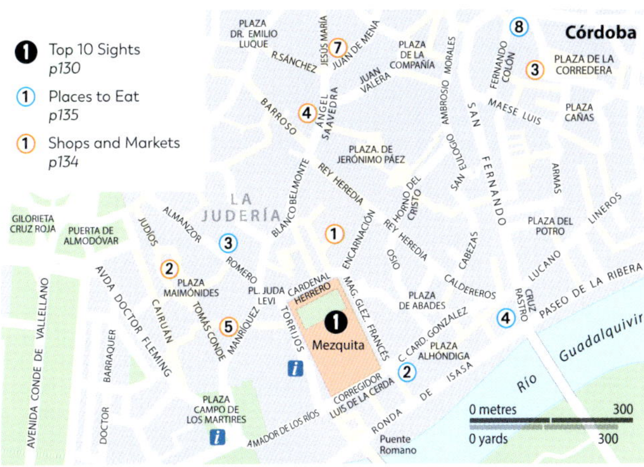

5 Cástulo

F2 Ctra Linares-Torreblascopedro (JV-3003) km 3.3

The ruins of this ancient city are situated in a strategic position in the Guadalquivir Valley. Cástulo is open to the public and is home to some immaculately preserved mosaics. The Monographic Museum of Cástulo *(Calle General Echagüe 2; museosdeandalucia.es)*, dedicated to this city and its history, is located 7 km (4 miles) away in Linares. All EU citizens can enter the museum free of charge.

6 Montoro

E2

Laid out on an undulating series of five hills at a bend in the river, this ancient town sports a Baroque tower and a handsome 15th-century bridge. Other sights include the Museo Arqueológico Municipal *(Plaza de Santa María de la Mota; 957 16 00 59; closed Mon)* and the eccentrically kitsch Casa de las Conchas *(C/Criado 17; 957 16 00 89)*, a shell-encrusted folly; contact the tourist office for tours, which are usually held on Saturday and Sunday.

7 Castillo de Almodóvar

D3 Almodóvar del Río, 25 km (16 miles) W of Córdoba

Hours vary, check website

castillodealmodovar.com

Originally the site of a Roman fortification, then a Moorish one, this present castle dates back to the 1300s, when it was embellished in Gothic style. Legend holds that ghosts of those who died while imprisoned here haunt the eight monolithic towers.

BAENA OLIVE OIL

This Córdoba Province town is famed for its olive oil, and you can catch its unmistakable fragrance as you enter the district. The Museo del Olivar y el Aceite *(C/Cañada 7; 957 69 16 41; open Tue–Sun)* is well worth a visit. It shows how each organically grown olive is carefully kept from bruising and the paste is extracted by the process of stone crushing.

8 Montilla

D3

The centre of Córdoba's wine making region, this town gave *amontillado* sherry its name (it means "in the style of Montilla"). The wine here is like sherry, but nuttier and more toasted. Since the region is hotter than around Jerez, the grapes ripen more intensely and the wines need no fortifying. You can taste the difference at Bodegas Alvear *(p80)*, founded in 1729.

9 Alcalá La Real

E3 ciudadesmedias.org

The 12th-century Fortaleza de la Mota *(p50)* dominates this once strategic town and is unique in Jaén Province in that its original Moorish castle was built by Badis Aben Habuz, the ruler of Granada. Although mostly in ruins, its original seven gates are still largely intact. Inside, built on the remains of a mosque, is the

Roman artifacts on display at the Monographic Museum of Cástulo

Gothic-Mudéjar church of Santo Domingo, which uses the former minaret as a bell tower.

10 Jaén

E3

This modern provincial capital is set off by the dramatic ramparts of the mighty Castillo de Santa Catalina *(p51)* and the grandeur of its double-towered cathedral *(Plaza Santa María; catedraldejaen.org)* by the famous Spanish architect Andrés de Vandelvira. Inside the cathedral are carved choir stalls and a museum of sacred art. The castle, now a parador, offers spectacular views of the city and its surrounding olive groves. Nearby, the Cruz del Castillo de Santa Catalina provides incredible panoramic views of Jaén and its environs. The city is also home to the Museo Provincial de Jaén *(Paseo de la Estación 29; museosde andalucia.es)*, which houses Spain's finest collection of 5th-century-BCE Iberian sculpture. Note that there is no admission charge for EU citizens.

Cruz del Castillo de Santa Catalina towering over Jaén

A MORNING WALK THROUGH BAEZA

Start your tour at the lovely **Plaza del Pópulo** *(p40)*. The tourist office is inside the fine Plateresque Casa del Pópulo. Next to it are the arches of the **Puerta de Jaén** *(p40)* and the Arco de Villalar, and in the centre is the **Fuente de los Leones**. Admire the ruined, yet elegant, lions and their eroded mistress, possibly Hannibal's wife.

Exiting the square to the left of the tourist office, continue southeast to the **Plaza Santa María** *(p40)* and the **cathedral** which has an extravagant choir screen by Bartolomé de Jaén.

Next, to the north, is the **Palacio de Jabalquinto** *(p51)*, with one of the most eccentric façades in the region, an example of Isabelline Plateresque style. It is now a university but you can visit its inner patio, then that of the Antigua Universidad next door. Opposite the palace, admire the well-preserved 13th-century church **Iglesia de Santa Cruz**.

Down the street, you can see the 1,000-year-old Moorish **Torre de los Aliatares** and around the corner, facing **Paseo de la Constitución** *(p63)*, **La Alhóndiga**, the old corn exchange, with its triple-tiered façade.

Lunch at traditional **Taberna El Pájaro** *(Portales Tundidores 5; 953 74 43 48; closed D Sun & Mon)* for its local fare and extensive wine list.

Shops and Markets

1. Meryan, Córdoba
D3 Calleja de las Flores 2
meryancor.com
A family-run business, Meryan is keeping Córdoba's famed leathercraft alive. Take your pick from a variety of handbags, accessories, frames and furniture.

2. Zoco Municipal, Córdoba
D3 C/Judios s/n
artesaniadecordoba.com
This historic house and patio has been converted into a co-op for local artists working in ceramics, leather, metal-works and woodwork.

3. Kuvo Plata, Córdoba
D3 C/Rodríguez Marín 18
kuvoplata.com
Located in the heart of Córdoba, close to the Templo Romano, this shop sells traditional silver jewellery inspired by Córdoba's history and culture.

4. La Oleoteca, Córdoba
D3 C/Ángel de Saavedra 8
laoleoteca.org
This gourmet store specializes in extra virgin olive oil and other regional products sourced from the local producers. Tasting and sampling of products is encouraged.

5. Baraka, Córdoba
D3 C/Manríquez
957 48 83 27
This is a good spot for quality souvenirs. Choose from ceramics, leather goods, glassware and other accessories, all handmade.

6. Ubedíes Artesanía con Esparto, Úbeda
F2 C/Real 45–7
ubediesartesania.com
Browse an innovative selection of items made with esparto grass, ranging from shoes to decorative items.

7. Monsieur Bourguignon, Córdoba
D3 C/Jesús María 11
605 98 75 84
A decadent shop offering an assortment of chocolates, biscuits and handmade sweets, which are almost too pretty to eat.

8. Galería de Vinos Caldos, Jaén
E3 C/Ceron 12 953 23 59 99
One of the area's best, this wine shop stocks regional wines, including those from Montilla *(p132)*.

9. Pottery Quarter, Úbeda
F2 C/Valencia
Úbeda is famous for its dark green pottery, fired in wood kilns over olive stones. Its intricate, pierced designs are Moorish-inspired and the artisanship is excellent.

10. Flea Market, Jaén
E3 Recinto Ferial, Avda de Granada
Thursday mornings see this street come to life with a catch-all market that can net you anything from pure junk to rare treasures.

Famous dark green pottery, Úbeda

Places to Eat

PRICE CATEGORIES

For a three-course meal for one with half a bottle of wine (or equivalent meal), taxes and extra charges.

€ under €30 €€ €30–€50 €€€ over €50

Beautiful dining area at Taberna Salinas, Córdoba

1. Casa Alfonso X El Sabio, Cazorla

G3 Placeta Consuelo Mendieta 2 Tue casalfonso.es · €€

Expertly prepared dishes and attentive service are on offer at this elegant restaurant. Opt for one of their *menús de degustación* (tasting menus).

2. Horno San Luis, Córdoba

D3 C/Cardenal Gonzalez 73 hornosanluis.com · €€

Housed in a historic *panaderia* (bread bakery), this stylish restaurant serves a varied cuisine.

3. El Churrasco, Córdoba

D3 C/Romero 16 Aug elchurrasco.com · €€€

With its sumptuous traditional fare, this is one of the city's popular restaurants. Try their eponymous *churrasco* – grilled pork loin with a spicy red pepper sauce.

4. Almudaina, Córdoba

D3 Plaza Campo Santo de los Martires 1 D Sun restaurantealmudaina.com · €€

Set in a 16th-century mansion, this is a great place to try traditional dishes, such as *pechuga de perniz en salsa* (partridge breasts in sauce).

5. Xavi Taberna, Baeza

F2 Portales Tundidores 8 D Tue & Wed xavitabernabaeza.com · €€

An excellent choice of seafood, plus a number of tasty vegetarian dishes, are available at this centrally located restaurant. The wine list is extensive and reasonably priced, and the service is both friendly and attentive.

6. Casa Rubio, Córdoba

E3 C/Puerta de Almodóvar 5 957 42 08 53 · €€

Known for its terrific tapas, this fine-dining restaurant serves a combination of nouvelle cuisine with the traditional flavours of the region.

7. Las Camachas, Montilla

D3 Ctra Madrid-Málaga, Avda de Europa 3 957 65 00 04 · €€

Fish dishes are a speciality here; opt for the hake loin with clams and prawns, paired with the delightful local wine.

8. Taberna Salinas, Córdoba

D3 C/Tundidores 3 Sun tabernasalinas.com · €

A bustling spot, this restaurant has dining rooms around a patio. Try the *naranjas picás con aceite y bacalao* (cod with orange and olive oil).

9. Panaceite, Jaén

E3 C/Bernabe Soriano 1 953 24 06 30 · €

If you're looking for a good selection of local specialities, head to Panaceite. The pork loin with onion marmalade is a must-try.

10. Mesón Navarro, Úbeda

F2 Plaza Ayuntamiento 2 953 75 73 95 · €

Try the *pinchitos* (kebabs) and *ochios* (rolls) at this local institution, where you can also enjoy views of the heritage city from the terrace.

STREETSMART

Scooting past Seville's spectacular cathedral

GETTING AROUND

Whether exploring Andalucía's great cities by foot or touring the surrounding provences by public transport, here is everything you need to know to navigate the region like a pro.

AT A GLANCE

PUBLIC TRANSPORT COSTS

SEVILLE
€5.00
Day Ticket
Bus and Train

CÓRDOBA
€1.55
Single Journey
Bus

MÁLAGA
€1.40
Single Journey
Bus

SPEED LIMITS

MOTORWAY
120 km/h (75 mph)

DUAL CARRIAGEWAYS
100 km/h (60 mph)

SECONDARY ROADS
90 km/h (55 mph)

URBAN AREAS
30 km/h (20 mph)

Arriving by Air

Andalucía is served by airports in Málaga, Almería, Granada-Jaén, Jerez and Seville. All are operated by **Aena.**

Málaga–Costa del Sol Airport (AGP) is Spain's fourth busiest. The much smaller Almería (LEI), Federico García Lorca Granada-Jaén (GRX), Jerez de Frontera (XRY) and Seville (SVQ) airports are served by domestic as well as European airlines, with chartered services increasing in the summer months. There are excellent public transport links from the airports to their nearest cities.
W aena.es

International Train Travel

Spain's international and domestic rail services are operated by state-run Red Nacional de Ferrocarriles Españoles (**Renfe**). For international train trips, it is advisable to purchase your ticket in advance from the Renfe website. **Eurail** also sells passes (to European non-residents and residents), which are valid on Renfe trains.

Eurail
W eurail.com
Renfe
W renfe.com

Regional and Local Trains

Renfe, along with some regional companies, operates a good train service throughout Andalucía. You can buy tickets online on the individual operators' websites or at stations. The fastest intercity services are the TALGO, Iryo, Avlo (Renfe's low-cost train line) and AVE (Renfe's full-service line), which link Madrid with Seville in two and a half hours. High-speed routes also link Barcelona with Seville and Málaga – both trips take five and a half hours.

The *largo recorrido* (long-distance) trains are cheaper but they are so slow that you usually need to travel overnight. Book at least a month in advance.

Regionales y cercanías (the regional and local services) are frequent, reliable and cheap.

Long-Distance Bus Travel

Often the cheapest and easiest way to travel around Andalucía is by coach. Coaches run frequently between most major cities and towns, and connect the region to the rest of Spain. The major coach stations in Andalucía are in Seville, Córdoba, Granada, Málaga and Almería. **Eurolines** links Andalucía to Portugal and there are international links to France, Austria, Switzerland, Belgium and the Netherlands.

Spain doesn't have a national coach company, but private regional coach companies operate routes around the country, the largest being **Alsa**.

Alsa
W alsa.es
Eurolines
W eurolines.com

Public Transport

Sightseeing and getting around Andalucía is best done on foot and by public transport. In most towns and cities, bus services generally suffice as the sole means of public transport; Seville, Málaga and Granada also have tram and metro systems. Jaén's tram system is due to open in 2025. Municipal or tourism websites in **Córdoba**, **Seville**, **Granada**, **Málaga**, **Almería** and **Cádiz** offer clear and up-to-date information about their public transport options.

Almería
W almeriaciudad.es
Cádiz
W tranviadecadizasanfernandoycarraca.es
Córdoba
W cordoba.es
Granada
W movilidadgranada.com
Málaga
W movilidad.malaga.eu
Seville
W visitasevilla.es

Tickets

The best place to purchase public transport tickets is at stations, either from windows or automatic machines. They are also available at newsagents. They come either in the form of a physical ticket or as a smart card, which can either hold a season ticket or be topped up with cash and used pay-as-you-go.

Metro

The **Metro de Sevilla** was designed to aid transport between the outer areas of Seville and the city centre. The system will eventually consist of four metro lines, which will provide easy access to bus and train stations.

The **Metro de Málaga** has two lines, which connect the outer suburbs to Guadalmedina and Atarazanas stations in the city centre.

The **Metropolitano de Granada** connects central Granada with the towns Armilla, Albolote and Maracena. All three metro systems offer frequent service and are an efficient way to avoid traffic, especially during peak hours.

Metropolitano de Granada
W metropolitanogranada.es
Metro de Málaga
W metromalaga.es
Metro de Sevilla
W metro-sevilla.es

Trams

Seville's city centre operates a modern tram system called the MetroCentro. It provides air-conditioned, rapid transport between San Bernardo station and Plaza Nueva in an otherwise largely pedestrian-only zone. An extension to the line is scheduled to open late 2027, connecting the network to Santa Justa train station.

Pay at the ticket machines at tram stops (or pass your contactless smart card over the reader on board) and press the green button to open the doors. MetroCentro trams run every 3 to 5 minutes and stop briefly at all designated stations.

Bus

Buses remain the most common mode of public transport throughout Andalucía, and are the easiest and cheapest way to get around Seville's main sights. However, they can sometimes follow an erratic timetable and many services do not run after 10pm. Bus routes can be found on the **TUSSAM** website.

TUSSAM
W tussam.es

Taxis

Throughout Andalucía, particularly in cities and towns, taxis are a reasonably priced way to get around if public transport isn't an option. Generally the journey starts with a flat fee and then increases depending on distance. Fares tend to be higher at night and during the weekend and public holidays. Surcharges usually apply for trips to airports, and bus and train stations.

For a more affordable option, visitors can use ride-sharing services, such as **BlaBlaCar**, to travel between cities. Apps such as Uber and Cabify are also popular.

BlaBlaCar
W blablacar.es

Driving

If you drive to Spain in your own car, you must carry the vehicle's registration document, a valid insurance certificate, a passport or a national identity card, and your driving licence at all times. You must also display a sticker on the back of the car showing its country of registration. Note that you risk on-the-spot fines if you do not carry a red warning triangle and a reflective jacket in the vehicle.

Spain has two types of motorway: *autopistas*, which are toll roads, and *autovías*, which are toll-free. You can establish whether a motorway is toll-free by the letters that prefix the number of the road: A = free; AP = toll.

Carreteras nacionales, Spain's main roads, have black-and-white signs and are designated by the letter N (Nacional) plus a number. Those with Roman numerals start at the Puerta del Sol in Madrid, and those with ordinary numbers have kilometre markers giving the distance from the provincial capital.

Carreteras comarcales, secondary roads, have a number preceded by the letter C. Other minor roads have numbers preceded by letters representing the name of the province, such as the GR-3301 in Granada.

Parking can be difficult, especially in the *pueblos blancos* where roads are narrow and there is limited availability. Instead, park outside the old town areas and walk in. Access to most Spanish cities with over 50,000 inhabitants is restricted. City centres are off-limits to vehicles that do not meet the emissions restrictions or do not display a government-issued emissions sticker.

Car Hire

In Andalucía all airports have several providers and there are many more smaller companies operating in city centres. To hire a car you'll need a valid, full driving licence, passport and credit card; some agencies will only accept customers over 21 or even 25 years.

The most popular car-hire companies in Spain are **Europcar**, **Avis** and **Hertz**. Fly-drive, an option for two or more travellers where car hire is included in the cost of your airfare, can be arranged by travel agents and tour operators. If you wish to hire a car locally for around a week or less, you will be able to arrange it with a local travel agent.

Avis
W avis.es

Europcar
W europcar.es

Hertz
W hertz.es

Rules of the Road

When using a car in Spain, drive on the right and use the left lane only for passing other vehicles.

If you have taken the wrong road, and it has a solid white line, turn round as indicated by a *cambio de sentido* sign. At crossings, give way to all on coming traffic, unless a sign indicates otherwise.

The speed limit is 120 km/h (75 mph) on motorways, 100 km/h (60 mph) on roads with more than one lane in each direction and 90 km/h (55 mph) on most rural roads, unless otherwise indicated. In urban areas, the speed limit varies, usually ranging from 20 km/h (12 mph) to 50 km/h (31 mph) depending on the type of road.

The blood-alcohol concentration (BAC) limit for drivers of private vehicles and cyclists is 0.5 mg/l and is strictly enforced. After a traffic accident, all those involved have to take a breath test.

Boats and Ferries

Ferries connect the Spanish mainland to the Balearic and Canary Islands, and to North Africa, Italy and the UK. All the important routes are served by car ferries. **Naviera Armas Trasmediterránea** operates a weekly service from Cádiz to the main ports of the Canary Islands. Always make an advance booking, especially in summer.

Naviera Armas Trasmediterránea
W armastrasmediterranea.com/en

Cycling

There are cycle lanes in most Andalucían cities. Seville has pedestrianized a main thoroughfare in the centre, creating a wide promenade, which allows for bikes. Rural Andalucía is bicycle-friendly, with an extensive network of back roads, though steep inclines can be testing for inexperienced cyclists.

For easier cycling, try the **Vias Verde** – "Greenway" – established throughout Spain by converting unused railway lines into recreational areas for leisure cycling, walking and horse riding. There are routes through each province in Andalucía. Bike hire is available in all the main towns and cities.

SEVICI is a self-service bike rental programme in Seville, with 2,500 bikes available 24 hours a day. Bikes can be hired free for 30 minutes and are charged per hour after that. Daily, weekly and annual rental subscriptions can be purchased online or through the app.

City traffic can be dangerous for cyclists. Helmets are highly recommended, and are obligatory for those under the age of 16.

SEVICI
W sevici.es

Vias Verde
W viasverdes.com

Walking

All of Andalucía's towns and cities are highly walkable, and many areas are pedestrianized. On foot, you can take in architectural details, absorb street life and peek into any church, shop or bar that catches your interest. Be aware that pavements can be narrow and uneven in historic centres. On hot days, try to keep to the shade and carry water with you at all times. Urban walking tours, often led by local guides, are a popular way to explore the history and hidden corners of Andalucían cities.

For the intrepid, long-distance trails criss cross Andalucía. One of the most established is the **GR7**, which starts in Tarifa and runs through Málaga and Granada, connecting the region with northern Spain, Andorra and France before linking, in Alsace, to the E5 path. Luggage transfer services, which will pick up or drop off bags from the start or end of your planned walk for a fee, are available.

The Camino Mozárabe is a waymarked route that forms part of the famous Camino de Santiago, also known as the Way of St James. The Andalucían section of the route runs for 396 km (246 miles) from Granada to Córdoba and then to Mérida. From Mérida, it connects with the Vía de la Plata, the northern route that ultimately leads to Santiago de Compostela.

GR7
W andalucia.com/rural/walking/gr7.htm

PRACTICAL INFORMATION

A little local know-how goes a long way in Andalucía. On these pages you can find all the essential advice and information you will need to make the most of your trip to the region.

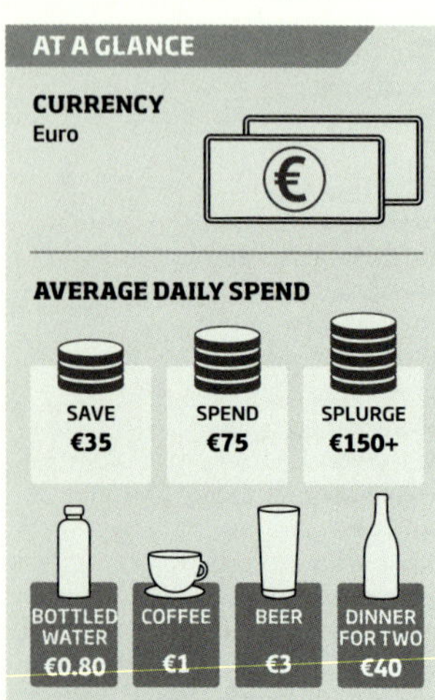

ESSENTIAL PHRASES

Hello	Hola
Goodbye	Adiós
Please	Por favor
Thank you	Gracias
Do you speak English?	¿Hablas inglés?
I don't understand...	No entiendo

ELECTRICITY SUPPLY

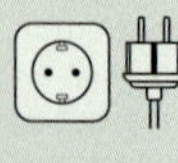

Power sockets are type F, fitting a two-prong, round-pin plug. Standard voltage is 230 volts.

Passports and Visas

For entry requirements, including visas, consult your nearest Spanish embassy or check the **Exteriores** website. Visitors from outside the European Economic Area (EEA), European Union (EU) and Switzerland need a valid passport to enter Spain. EEA, EU and Swiss nationals can use identity cards instead.

Citizens of the UK, US, Canada, Australia and New Zealand do not need a visa for stays of up to three months but must apply in advance for the European Travel Information and Authorization System (**ETIAS**). Visitors from other countries may also require an ETIAS, so check before travelling. EU nationals do not need a visa or an ETIAS.

ETIAS
W etiasvisa.com
Exteriores
W exteriores.gob.es

Government Advice

Now more than ever, it is important to consult both your and the Spanish government's advice before travelling. The **UK Foreign & Commonwealth Office**, the **US Department of State**, the **Australian Department of Foreign Affairs and Trade**, and the Exteriores website offer the latest information on security, health and local regulations.

Australian Department of Foreign Affairs and Trade
W smartraveller.gov.au
UK Foreign & Commonwealth Office
W gov.uk/foreign-travel-advice
US Department of State
W travel.state.gov

Customs Information

You can find information on the laws relating to goods and currency taken in or out of Spain on the **Turespaña** (Spain's national tourist board) website.

For EU citizens there are no limits on most goods carried in or out of Spain as long as they are for personal use. There are, however, exceptions that include firearms and weapons, some types of food and plants, and endangered species.

Non-EU citizens are allowed to import 200 cigarettes and a litre of spirits per adult, and can get a refund on Spain's 21 per cent sales tax (VAT, known here as IVA) on purchases over €90.15 – do this at the airport when leaving *(p145)*.

Turespaña
W spain.info

Insurance

We recommend that you take out a comprehensive insurance policy covering theft, loss of belongings, medical care, cancellations and delays, and read the small print carefully.

EU citizens are eligible for free emergency medical care in Spain provided they have a valid European Health Insurance Card (EHIC); UK citizens need a Global Health Insurance Card (**GHIC**).

GHIC
W ghic.org.uk

Vaccinations

No vaccinations are necessary.

Money

Most urban establishments accept major credit, debit and prepaid currency cards. Contactless payments are common in cities, but it's always a good idea to carry cash for smaller items and to buy some transport tickets. ATMs are widely available, although many charge for cash withdrawals.

Spain does not have a big tipping culture, but it's appreciated and common to round up the bill.

Travellers with Specific Requirements

Spain is well equipped when it comes to accessibility, but it is still advisable to call hotels and restaurants ahead of time and ask about the specific amenities available. The Confederación Española de Personas con Discapacidad Física y Orgánica (**COCEMFE**) and **Accessible Spain** provide information and tailored itineraries for those with reduced mobility, sight and hearing.

Spain's public transport system generally caters for all passengers, providing wheelchairs, adapted toilets and ramps. All public transport in Seville can accommodate wheelchair users comfortably. Airports offer reserved car parking, as well as other supportive facilities. Metro maps in Braille are available from the Organización Nacional de Ciegos (**ONCE**), and audio guides are often provided at major attractions.

Accessible Spain
W accessiblespain travel.com

COCEMFE
W cocemfe.es

ONCE
W once.es

Language

Castellano (Castilian) is Spain's primary language and is spoken in Andalucía. English is widely spoken in the cities and other tourist spots, but the same cannot always be said for rural areas. Mastering a few phrases in *Castellano* will go down well with locals.

Opening Hours

Typical business hours are Monday–Saturday 9:30am–1:30pm and 4:30–8pm. Major shopping centres and department stores are open all day 10am–9pm. In the high season in coastal areas many stay open until after 10pm. Smaller stores usually close by 3pm on Saturday.

Most museums, public buildings and many shops close early or for the day on public holidays.

Situations can change quickly and unexpectedly. Always check before visiting attractions and hospitality venues for up-to-date opening hours and booking requirements.

Personal Security

Andalucía is a safe and welcoming region but petty crime does take place. Pickpockets work in known tourist areas, stations and busy streets. Use common sense and be alert to your surroundings, and you should enjoy a stress-free trip.

AT A GLANCE

EMERGENCY NUMBERS

GENERAL EMERGENCY

112

TIME ZONE

CET/CEST: Central European Summer time (CEST) runs last Sunday in March to last Sunday in October.

TAP WATER

Tap water in Andalucía is safe to drink unless stated otherwise.

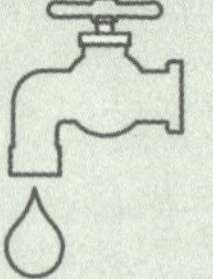

WEBSITES AND APPS

Andalucía
Offers information from Andalucía's tourism board *(www.andalucia.org)*.

España
Spain's official tourism website *(www.spain.info)*.

Moovit
A route-planning app.

WiFi Map
Finds free Wi-Fi hotspots near you *(www.wifimap.io)*.

If you do have anything stolen, report the crime within 24 hours to the nearest police station and take ID with you. Get a copy of the crime report *(denuncia)* to make an insurance claim. Contact your embassy if you have your passport stolen, or in the event of a serious crime.

Andalucíans are very accepting of all people, regardless of their race, gender or sexuality. Homosexuality was legalized in Spain in 1979 and in 2007, the government recognized same-sex marriage and adoption rights for same-sex couples. That being said, the Catholic Church still holds a lot of sway here and some conservative attitudes prevail, especially outside of urban areas. If you do feel unsafe, the **Safe Space Alliance** can pinpoint your nearest place of refuge.

Safe Space Alliance
W safespacealliance.com

Health

Spain has a world-class healthcare system. Emergency medical care in Spain is free for all UK and EU citizens with a valid EHIC or GHIC *(p143)*. If you have an EHIC or GHIC, be sure to present this as soon as possible. You may have to pay after treatment and reclaim the money later.

For visitors coming from outside the UK or EU, payment of medical expenses is the patient's responsibility, so it is important to arrange comprehensive insurance before travelling.

Seek medical supplies and advice for minor ailments from a pharmacy *(farmacia)*, identifiable by a green or red cross. When closed, each pharmacy displays a card in the window showing the address of the nearest all-night pharmacy (or look online for Farmácias de Guardia to locate the nearest one).

Smoking, Alcohol and Drugs

Smoking is banned in enclosed public spaces and is a fineable offence, although you can still smoke on the terraces of bars and restaurants. Spain has a relaxed attitude towards alcohol consumption, but it is frowned upon to be visibly drunk.

Most recreational drugs are illegal, and possession of even a very small quantity can lead to an extremely hefty fine. Amounts that suggest an intent to supply drugs to other people can lead to custodial sentences.

ID

By law you must carry identification with you at all times in Spain. A photocopy of your passport should suffice, but you may be asked to report to a police station with the original document, if stopped by the police.

Responsible Tourism

The climate crisis is having a big impact on the region, with droughts and heatwaves becoming more frequent. Do your bit by taking quick showers and reusing towels if staying in a hotel. Andalucía is also at risk of wildfires so be careful when disposing of cigarette butts; starting a fire, even if accidental, is a criminal offence.

Visiting Churches and Cathedrals

Generally, entrance to churches is free; though a fee may apply to enter special areas, like cloisters. Out of respect, ensure that you are dressed modestly

Bullfighting

Corridas (bullfights) are widely held in Andalucía. Supporters argue that the bulls are bred for the industry and would be killed as calves were it not for bullfighting, while some charities say that it's cruel and organize protests throughout the country. If you do decide to attend a corrida, bear in mind that it's better to see a big-name matador because they are more likely to make a clean and quick kill. The audience will make their disapproval evident if not.

Mobile Phones and Wi-Fi

Cities and towns across Andalucía are provided with plenty of Wi-Fi hotspots. Visit the **WiFi Map** website to find free hotspots near you.

Visitors with EU tariffs can use their devices without being affected by roaming charges. Some UK networks have reintroduced roaming charges; check with your provider before travelling.

WiFi Map
W wifimap.io

Postal Services

Spanish mail is efficient, reliable and fast. **Correos** is the national mail service; note that office opening hours vary. Buy stamps from the post office or vending machines.

Correos
W correos.es

Visitor Information

There are official tourist information booths at the airport and in cities and bigger towns. Here you can get maps and city passes that allow discounts on sights, arrange hop on/hop off bus tours, or find out what's on locally. The official websites for the **Andalucía** and **España** tourism boards offer further information.

Some cities offer a visitor's pass or discount card that can be used for free or reduced-price entry to events and museums, and even discounts at participating restaurants. Passes are not free, so consider carefully how many of the offers you are likely to take advantage of before purchasing one of them.

Andalucía
W andalucía.org
España
W spain.info

Taxes and Refunds

IVA (value added tax) in mainland Spain tends to be 21 per cent, but with lower rates for certain goods and services.

Under certain conditions, non-EU citizens can claim a rebate of these taxes. Retailers can give you a form to fill out, which you can then present to a customs officer at your point of departure or validate it at one of the self-service machines found at Spain's main ports and airports.

PLACES TO STAY

Accommodation in Andalucía suits all styles and budgets, from luxury hotels and historic buildings to rural retreats and beachfront apartments. Summer brings high temperatures, making beaches and mountains popular but also pricier. Conversely, cities like Seville, Córdoba and Granada see lower rates during the hot season. Choosing where to stay depends on how you plan to explore Andalucía; whether you're city-hopping, hitting the coast or escaping to the countryside, you'll find options to suit your needs.

PRICE CATEGORIES
For a standard double room per night (with breakfast if included), taxes and extra charges.

€ under €100
€€ €100–€200
€€€ over €200

Seville

Hotel Ateneo

Plaza Fernando de Herrera 6 hotelateneo sevilla.com · €€€

Set in a former palace in Seville, this Renaissance-style hotel is all about opulence. Its suites are lavish, with gilded furniture and twinkling chandeliers, and there's a lovely central patio and wood-panelled library. The best bit? The location. You'll be just a stone's throw from Casa de Pilatos and the cathedral.

Hotel Casa de Colón

C/Hernando Colón, 3 hotelcasadecolon.com · €€

Nestled in the historic heart of Seville (the Giralda is just three minutes away on foot), this beautiful boutique hotel is in an old manor house. Many 19th-century features are still intact, including intricately tiled walls and blue stained-glass windows. The Pazos family, who run the hotel, are wonderfully welcoming, and will cater to your every need.

Triana House Boutique Hotel

C/Rodrigo de Triana 94 trianahouse.com · €€€

Found in Seville's lively Triana neighbourhood, this gorgeous boutique hotel is inspired by Moorish-style aesthetics. Each of the rooms, created by Sevillian designer Armaro Sanchez de Moya, is decorated with antique furniture and beautiful tiling, and are all blessed with luxury Vispring mattresses to ensure a restful night.

Hotel San Gil

C/Parras 28 hotelsangil.es · €

In the Macarena neighbourhood, Hotel San Gil offers a clean and comfortable retreat. Highlights include a rooftop pool and bar, and a serene interior garden. While situated in a quieter part of Seville, the hotel is just a convenient ten-minute stroll from the city's main attractions.

Hotel Monte Carmelo

C/Virgen de la Victoria 7 hotelmontecarmelo.com · €€

Exceptional service with a smile is a given at this four-star hotel in the Los Remedios area of Seville. It offers great value for money, too, with modern, functional and bright rooms just five minutes' walk from the cathedral.

Hotel Doña Blanca

Plaza Padre Jerónimo de Córdoba 14 donablanca.com · €

Ideally located in front of the 14th-century Church of Santa Catalina, this charming, family-run hotel occupies a traditional Sevillian mansion, with rooms set around a gorgeous fountain-filled patio. It offers 24-hour service, car hire and even a grand library for guests. With accessible facilities and wheelchair hire, it's more than just the location that makes this a great choice for those with reduced mobility.

Sevilla and Huelva Provinces

Hotel Vereda Real

Urbanización Brisas del Aljarafe, Valencina de la Concepción hotelveredareal.com · €–€€

Vereda Real is a tranquil hotel set among gardens and olive groves, with a pool open during the summer. It's an ideal base for those wishing to explore further afield, just 9 km (5.5 miles) from Seville's cathedral and within an hour's drive of Doñana National Park and Huelva's beaches.

Casona de Calderón

Plaza de Cervantes 16, Osuna casonacalderon.es · €

This four-star boutique hotel, in the centre of Osuna, is charmingly rustic, featuring stone floors and exposed beams. It's a great place to relax, too, with a leafy courtyard and patio area, complete with a peaceful fountain.

Hotel Torre de la Reina

Paseo de la Alameda, Torre de la Reina, Guillena torredelareina.com · €€

Housed in a 13th-century fortress in the Sevillian countryside, this luxury boutique hotel features a seasonal pool and a farm-to-fork restaurant. Located about 15 km (9.5 miles) from Seville city centre, it also offers easy access to charming towns like Carmona and Ecija, as well as the scenic Sierra Norte Natural Park.

Hotel Convento Aracena

C/Jesús y María 19, hotelconventoaracena.es · €€

Luxury and comfort meet at this four-star hotel set in a beautifully restored 17th-century convent in the heart of enchanting Aracena. Facilities include a fully equipped gym, indoor and outdoor pools, and a spa with a range of facilities and treatments.

Hotel Ardea Purpurea

Camino Vereda de los Labrados, Villamanrique de la Condesa ardeapurpurea.com · €€

Award-winning and truly original accommodation in the heart of Doñana Park, this hotel offers everything from simple rooms to marsh huts, and even a chestnut-thatched igloo. Guests can enjoy a range of activities, including a lynx photography trail, horse riding and bird-watching, plus an outdoor sand pool perfect for leisurely swims in nature. The on-site restaurant serves generous portions of hearty, rustic-style food.

Hotel Posada de Valdezufre

Avenida Santa Marina 1, Valdezufre valdezufre.es · €€

A neat three-star hotel nestled in the mountains surrounding Aracena, set amid beautiful gardens with a seasonal outdoor pool. With free on-site parking, it's a great base for exploring nearby attractions, including the Gruta de las Maravillas, Aracena Castle and the Rio Tinto mines.

Málaga and Cádiz Provinces

Hotel Palacio de la Duquesa

C/Espíritu Santo 13, Ronda palaciodeladuquesa.com · €€

This four-star hotel in historic Ronda is a peaceful oasis, set within 2,000 sq m (21,500 sq ft) of lush gardens. Guests can enjoy an exclusive pool and a restaurant with lovely views. Ideally located next to the Iglesia del Espíritu Santo, it's just a 10-minute walk from the Arab Baths and the iconic Puente Nuevo.

Hotel La Fuente de la Higuera

Partido de los Frontones s/n, Ronda hotellafuente.com · €€€

Housed inside a reformed mill and surrounded by olive groves and fruit and nut trees, this four-star hotel is set apart thanks to its stunning views of the Ronda countryside. Elegant rooms add to the charm, as does the on-site restaurant, known for its great food made from ingredients fresh from the hotel's gardens.

Hotel Convento Cister

C/Tomás de Cózar 2, Málaga ldhoteles.com/hoteles/ld-convento-cister malaga • €€

This thoughtfully restored 16th-century convent, once home to Cistercian nuns, offers a unique retreat for city-slickers. Located in the centre of Málaga, close to the main tourist and shopping districts, the hotel combines historic charm with modern comfort. The rooms are elegantly contemporary, an appealing contrast to the preserved original features.

Hotel Málaga Nostrum

C/Herman Hesse 17, Málaga hotelmalaga nostrum.com • €

A budget hotel halfway between the airport and the vibrant hub of Málaga. Rooms are functional and clean, and what it lacks in location is compensated by an amazing rooftop pool and terrace. It also has a car park facility and is fully accessible for people with mobility issues.

Casa Palacio María Luisa

C/Torneria 22, Jerez casapalaciomaria luisa.com • €€€

Staying at this five-star hotel is like going back in time to 19th-century Jerez, when members of the aristocracy frequented the casino formerly located here. In its place Hotel Casa Palacio María Luisa offers luxury five-star elegance, with 21 art-filled rooms and suites, a rooftop plunge pool, chic bar and gourmet in-house restaurant. If you're after somewhere opulent, this is it.

Hotel Jerez Centro

C/Marqués de la Casa-Domecq, 13 barcelo.com/es-es/hotel-jerez-centro • €€€

A four-star city-centre hotel housed in an emblematic historic building surrounded by orange trees and palms. Just a short walk to the main attractions in the historical centre of town, it has nearly 100 stylish, air-conditioned rooms with minibars and free Wi-Fi. Enjoy a delicious gourmet buffet breakfast, 24-hour reception and four modern meeting rooms, ideal for upscale urban stays.

Granada and Almería Provinces

Hotel Casa 1800

C/Benalua 11, Granada hotelcasa1800 granada.com • €€ (Apr & May €€€)

Nestled at the foot of the Alhambra, this charming three-star hotel was once the 16th-century residence of the Lords of Cañaveral, Counts of Benalúa. It has a Castilian feel with dark wood furnishings and terracotta tile floors. And you'll certainly feel like a noble thanks to touches like Egyptian cotton sheets, fresh flowers and the option to have breakfast served in bed.

Hotel Casa Morisca

Cuesta de la Victoria 9, Granada hotelcasa morisca.com • €€

This award-winning three-star hotel is housed inside a 15th-century Moorish residence in Granada's Albaicín district. Built around a central courtyard and fountain, it features stucco arches, wooden balconies and intricately tiled floors. The city centre is just a few minutes' walk away, as is the majestic Alhambra.

Hotel Atenas Granada

C/Gran Vía de Colón 38, Granada hostal atenas.com • €

Exploring Granada on a budget? This hotel offers excellent value right in the city's vibrant centre. Just a five-minute stroll from landmarks like the Basilica de San Juan de Dios, the cathedral, and the Alcaicería Silk Market, it's also surrounded by bars and restaurants. Accommodation options range from simple singles and doubles to charming, characterful apartments.

Hotel Cala Arena

C/Correo 13, San José hotelcalaarena.com • €€

Just 50 m (164 ft) from the beach at San José, this sustainable, family-run hotel offers a perfect base for exploring the Cabo de Gata Natural Park, and has wonderful sea views. The hotel also features an advanced aerothermal heating and cooling system, and solar panels, ideal for eco-conscious travellers. Note there's a minimum stay of two to three nights during the high season.

Hostal Avenida

Glorieta de España 10, Tabernas hostalavenida.es · €

This simple hotel offers a warm welcome in the middle of the Almerían desert and is a great base for visiting the nearby attractions of Fort Bravo or Paque Oasys. It's great for outdoor adventurers, too, with hiking, cycling, quadbiking and horse-riding routes nearby.

Córdoba and Jaén Provinces

Hotel Las Casas de la Judería

C/Tomas Conde 10, Córdoba lascasasdelajuderiadecordoba.com · €€

This four-star hotel is in a 16th-century mansion in the centre of Córdoba's old Jewish quarter. The rooms are spacious and light, and guests can enhance their stay with thoughtful extras, such as tours of the city, massages and poolside cocktails. There's even a pillow menu to choose from to ensure the perfect night's sleep.

Hostal Patios del Orfebre

C/Tejón y Marín 1, Córdoba patiosdelorfebre.es · €€

In the heart of Córdoba's historic Jewish quarter, this hotel occupies a protected 16th-century *casa patio* with original features. Rooms surround arcaded courtyards, including one with a 4th-century BCE archaeological site. That's not to say there are no mod cons here: expect porcelain floors, en-suite rain showers, and soundproofing throughout.

Hotel Casa Museo de la Mezquita

Plaza de Santa Catalina 1, Córdoba hotelmezquita.com · €€

Simple but stylish, this hotel, formerly a 16th-century mansion, is right in front of Córdoba's Mezquita, making it a great base for exploring. Rooms are comfortable and light, and the service is warm and friendly.

Hotel Puerta de la Luna

Canónigo Melgares Raya s/n, Baeza hotelpuertadelaluna.com · €€

A welcoming, family-run hotel in a 16th-century mansion just steps from Baeza's cathedral. Modern, airy rooms are surrounded by beautiful gardens and a serene pool, creating a relaxed and inviting atmosphere. What truly sets this hotel apart, though, is its personal touch; staff here are committed to impeccable, friendly service, and nothing is ever too much trouble. Don't miss the on-site restaurant; dinner here is a must.

Parador Jaen

Castillo de Santa Catalina s/n, Jaén paradores.es/en/parador-de-jaen · €€€

Standing on the hill of Santa Catalina, next to archaeological remains from the Phoenician period, this hotel has stunning views of the surrounding area. While the building itself is a historic monument, it seamlessly combines heritage with modern comfort. Guests can enjoy contemporary amenities such as free parking and even an on-site electric vehicle charging station.

Hotel María de Molina

Plaza del Ayuntamiento, Ubeda hotelmariamolina.com · €

This charming, three-star hotel is located right in the centre of Ubeda. It was once a 16th-century palace, and has plenty of original features, including an interior patio, fountain and beautiful marble staircase. Rooms are basic but light and have all the conveniences necessary, such as air-conditioning, a television and free Wi-Fi.

INDEX

Page numbers in **bold** refer to main entries.

D

E

F

G

H

I

J

L

R

S

PHRASE BOOK

In an Emergency

Help!	**¡Socorro!**	*soh-koh-roh*
Stop!	**¡Pare!**	*pah-reh*
Call…	**¡Llame a…**	*yah-meh ah*
…a doctor!	**…un médico!**	*oon meh-dee-koh*
…an ambulance!	**…una ambulancia!**	*oonah ahm-boo -lahn-thee-ah*
…the police!	**…la policía!**	*lah poh-lee-thee-ah*
…the fire brigade!	**…los bomberos!**	*lohs bohm-beh-rohs*
Where is…	**¿Dónde está…**	*dohn-deh ehs-tah*
…the nearest telephone?	**…el teléfono más próximo?**	*ehl teh-leh-foh-noh mahs prohx-ee moh*
…the nearest hospital?	**…el hospital más próximo?**	*ehl ohs pee-tahl mahs prohx-ee-moh*

Communication Essentials

Yes	**Sí**	*see*
No	**No**	*noh*
Please	**Por favor**	*pohr fah-vohr*
Thank you	**Gracias**	*grah-thee-ahs*
Excuse me	**Perdone**	*pehr-doh-neh*
Hello	**Hola**	*oh-lah*
Goodbye	**Adiós**	*ah-dee-ohs*
Good night	**Buenas noches**	*bweh-nahs noh-chehs*
Morning	**La mañana**	*lah mah-nyah-nah*
Afternoon/Evening	**La tarde**	*lah tahr-deh*
Yesterday	**Ayer**	*ah-yehr*
Today	**Hoy**	*oy*
Tomorrow	**Mañana**	*mah-nya-nah*
Here	**Aquí**	*ah-kee*
There	**Allí**	*ah-yee*
What?	**¿Qué?**	*keh*
When?	**¿Cuándo?**	*kwahn-doh*
Why?	**¿Por qué?**	*pohr-keh*
Where?	**¿Dónde?**	*dohn-deh*

Useful Phrases

How are you?	**¿Cómo está usted?**	*koh-moh ehs-tah oos-tehd*
Very well, thank you	**Muy bien, gracias**	*mwee bee-ehn grah-thee-ahs*
Pleased to meet you.	**Encantado de conocerle.**	*ehn-kahn-tah-doh deh thehr-leh*
See you soon	**Hasta pronto**	*ahs-tah-prohn-toh*
That's fine	**Está bien**	*ehs-tah bee-ehn*
Where is/are…?	**¿Dónde está/están…?**	*dohn-deh ehs-tah/ehs-tahn*
How far is it to…?	**Cuántos metros/ kilómetros hay de aquí a…?**	*kwahn-tohs meh-trohs/kee-loh-meh-trohs eye deh ah-kee ah*
Which way to…?	**¿Por dónde se va a…?**	*pohr dohn-deh seh bah ah*
Do you speak English?	**¿Habla inglés?**	*ah-blah een-glehs*
I don't understand	**No comprendo**	*noh kohm-prehn-doh*
Could you speak more slowly please?	**¿Puede hablar más despacio por favor?**	*pweh-deh ah-blahr mahs dehs -pah-thee-oh pohr fah-vohr*
I'm sorry	**Lo siento**	*loh see-ehn-toh*

Shopping

How much does this cost?	**¿Cuánto cuesta esto?**	*kwahn-toh kwehs-tah ehs-toh*
I would like…	**Me gustaría…**	*meh goos-ta-ree-ah*
Do you have…?	**¿Tienen…?**	*tee-yeh-nehn*
Do you take cards?	**¿Aceptan tarjetas?**	*ah-thehp-tahn tahr-heh-tahs*
What time do you open/close?	**¿A qué hora abren/cierran?**	*ah keh oh-rah ah-brehn/ thee-ehr-rahn*
expensive	**caro**	*kahr-oh*
cheap	**barato**	*bah-rah-toh*
size, clothes	**talla**	*tah-yah*
size, shoes	**número**	*noo-mehr-oh*
bakery	**la panadería**	*pah-nah-deh ree-ah*
bank	**el banco**	*bahn-koh*
bookshop	**la librería**	*lee-breh-ree-ah*
chemist's	**la farmacia**	*ahr-mah-thee-ah*
market	**el mercado**	*mehr-kah-doh*
newsagent's	**el kiosko de prensa**	*kee-ohs-koh deh prehn-sah*
post office	**la oficina de correos**	*oh-fee thee-nah deh kohr-reh-ohs*
shoe shop	**la zapatería**	*thah-pah-teh-ree-ah*
supermarket	**el super-mercado**	*soo-pehr-mehr-kah-doh*

Staying in a Hotel

Do you have a vacant room?	**¿Tiene una habitación libre?**	*tee-eh-neh oo-nah ah-bee- tah-thee-ohn lee-breh*
double room	**habitación doble**	*ah-bee-tah-thee-ohn doh-bleh*
with double bed	**con cama de matrimonio**	*kohn kah-mah deh mah-tree-moh-nee-oh*
twin room	**habitación con dos camas**	*ah-bee-tah-thee-ohn kohn dohs kah-mahs*
single room	**habitación individual**	*ah-bee-tah-thee-ohn een-dee-vee-doo-ahl*
room with a bath	**habitación con baño**	*ah-bee-tah-thee-ohn kohn bah-nyoh*
key	**la llave**	*yah-veh*
I have a reservation	**Tengo una habitación reservada**	*tehn-goh oo-na ah-bee-tah-thee -ohn reh-sehr-bah-dah*

Eating Out

Have you got a table for…?	**¿Tiene mesa para…?**	*tee-eh-neh meh-sah pah-rah*

I want to reserve a table	**Quiero reservar una mesa**	*kee-eh-roh reh-sehr-bahr oo-nah meh-sah*
the bill	**La cuenta**	*kwehn-tah*
I am a vegetarian	**Soy vegetariano/a**	*soy beh-heh-tah-ree-ah-no/na*
waitress/ waiter	**camarera/ camarero**	*kah-mah-reh-rah/ kah-mah-reh-roh*
menu	**la carta**	*kahr-tah*
fixed-price menu	**menú del día**	*meh-noo dehl dee-ah*
wine list	**la carta de vinos**	*kahr-tah deh bee-nohs*
glass	**un vaso**	*bah-soh*
knife	**un cuchillo**	*koo-chee-yoh*
fork	**un tenedor**	*teh-neh-dohr*
spoon	**una cuchara**	*koo-chah-rah*
breakfast	**el desayuno**	*deh-sah-yoo-noh*
lunch	**la comida/ el almuerzo**	*koh-mee-dah/ ahl-mwehr-thoh*
dinner	**la cena**	*theh-nah*
main course	**el primer plato**	*pree-mehr plah-toh*
starters	**los entremeses**	*ehn-treh-meh-ses*
dish of the day	**el plato del día**	*plah-toh dehl dee-ah*
coffee	**el café**	*kah-feh*

Menu Decoder

al horno	*ahl ohr-noh*	baked
asado	*ah-sah-doh*	roast
el aceite	*ah-thee-eh-teh*	oil
las aceitunas	*ah-theh-toon-ahs*	olives
el agua mineral	*ah-gwa mee-neh-rahl*	mineral water
sin gas/con gas	*seen gas/kohn gas*	still/sparkling
el ajo	*ah-hoh*	garlic
el arroz	*ahr-rohth*	rice
el azúcar	*ah-thoo-kahr*	sugar
la carne	*kahr-neh*	meat
la cebolla	*theh-boh-yah*	onion
el chorizo	*choh-ree-thoh*	spicy sausage
frito	*free-toh*	fried
la fruta	*froo-tah*	fruit
los frutos secos	*froo-tohs seh-kohs*	nuts
las gambas	*gahm-bahs*	prawns
el helado	*eh-lah-doh*	ice cream
el huevo	*oo-eh-voh*	egg
el jamón serrano	*hah-mohn sehr-rah-noh*	cured ham
la langosta	*lahn-gohs-tah*	lobster
la leche	*leh-cheh*	milk
la mantequilla	*mahn-teh-kee-yah*	butter
los mariscos	*mah-rees-kohs*	seafood
la naranja	*nah-rahn-hah*	orange
el pan	*pahn*	bread
el pastel	*pahs-tehl*	pastry
las patatas	*pah-tah-tahs*	potatoes
el pescado	*pehs-kah-doh*	fish
la pimienta	*pee-mee-yehn-tah*	pepper
el pollo	*poh-yoh*	chicken
el postre	*pohs-treh*	dessert
el queso	*keh-soh*	cheese
la sal	*sahl*	salt
la salsa	*sahl-sah*	sauce
seco	*seh-koh*	dry
la sopa	*soh-pah*	soup
la tarta	*tahr-tah*	pie/cake
el té	*teh*	tea
el vinagre	*bee-nah-greh*	vinegar

Numbers

0	**cero**	*theh-roh*
1	**uno**	*oo-noh*
2	**dos**	*dohs*
3	**tres**	*trehs*
4	**cuatro**	*kwa-troh*
5	**cinco**	*theen-koh*
6	**seis**	*says*
7	**siete**	*see-eh-teh*
8	**ocho**	*oh-choh*
9	**nueve**	*nweh-veh*
10	**diez**	*dee-ehth*
11	**once**	*ohn-theh*
12	**doce**	*doh-theh*
13	**trece**	*treh-theh*
14	**catorce**	*kah-tohr-theh*
15	**quince**	*keen-theh*
16	**dieciséis**	*dee-eh-thee-seh-ees*
17	**diecisiete**	*dee-eh-thee-see-eh-teh*
18	**dieciocho**	*dee-eh-thee-oh-choh*
19	**diecinueve**	*dee-eh-thee-nweh-veh*
20	**veinte**	*beh-een-teh*
21	**veintiuno**	*beh-een-tee-oo-noh*
22	**veintidós**	*beh-een-tee-dohs*
30	**treinta**	*treh-een-tah*
31	**treinta y uno**	*treh-een-tah ee oo-noh*
40	**cuarenta**	*kwah-rehn-tah*
50	**cincuenta**	*theen-kwehn-tah*
60	**sesenta**	*seh-sehn-tah*
70	**setenta**	*seh-tehn-tah*
80	**ochenta**	*oh-chehn-tah*
90	**noventa**	*noh-vehn-tah*
100	**cien**	*thee-ehn*
101	**ciento uno**	*thee-ehn-toh oo-noh*
200	**doscientos**	*dohs-thee-ehn-tohs*
500	**quinientos**	*khee-nee-ehn-tohs*
1,000	**mil**	*meel*

Time

one minute	**un minuto**	*oon mee-noo-toh*
one hour	**una hora**	*oo-na oh-rah*
half an hour	**media hora**	*meh-dee-a oh-rah*
Monday	**lunes**	*loo-nehs*
Tuesday	**martes**	*mahr-tehs*
Wednesday	**miércoles**	*mee-ehr-koh-lehs*
Thursday	**jueves**	*hoo-weh-vehs*
Friday	**viernes**	*bee-ehr-nehs*
Saturday	**sábado**	*sah-bah-doh*
Sunday	**domingo**	*doh-meen-goh*

ACKNOWLEDGMENTS

This edition updated by

Contributor Lynnette McCurdy Bastida

Senior Editor Kiron Gill

Senior Designers Katie Cavanagh, Stuti Tiwari

Project Editor Anuroop Sanwalia

Project Art Editor Divyanshi Shreyaskar

Editors Abhidha Lakhera, Eleanora Reeves, Sarah Mathew (Assistant Editor)

Proofreader Kathryn Glendenning

Indexer Helen Peters

Picture Research Deputy Manager Virien Chopra

Senior Picture Researcher Nishwan Rasool

Assistant Picture Research Administrator Manpreet Kaur

Publishing Assistant Simona Velikova

Jacket Designer Divyanshi Shreyaskar, Katie Cavanagh

Jacket Picture Researcher Naomi McMullen

Project Cartographer Ashif

Senior Cartographer James Macdonald

Cartography Manager Suresh Kumar

Pre-Production Coordinator Tanveer Zaidi

Pre-Production Designer Rohit Rojal

Pre-Production Image Editor Nityanand Kumar, Vikram Singh

Pre-Production Manager Balwant Singh

Pre-Production Image Manager Pankaj Sharma

Production Controller Kariss Ainsworth

Deputy Managing Editor Dharini Ganesh

Managing Editor Beverly Smart

Managing Art Editor Gemma Doyle

Senior Managing Art Editor Priyanka Thakur

Editorial Director Hollie Teague

Art Director Maxine Pedliham

Publishing Director Georgina Dee

DK would like to thank the following for their contribution to the previous editions: Jeffrey Kennedy, Chris Moss

The publisher would like to thank the following for their kind permission to reproduce their photographs:

Key: a-above; b-below/bottom; c-center; f-far; l-left; r-right; t-top

Adobe Stock: Autumn Sky 21b, Horváth Botond 5, DavidShaun 30-31t, dudlajzov 20, elroce 12cr, Kirk Fisher 29tl, jorgesierra 99, Lucía 83, Mathieu 48-49t, mrks_v 52, TOimages 16tr, Anibal Trejo 89, Madrugada Verde 68-69t, yujie 26, Zied 14

Alamy Stock Photo: A.J.D. Foto Ltd. 10tl, Mauricio Abreu 17, 50, age fotostock / J.D. Dallet 128, age fotostock / Rafael Campillo 79, Album 9br, Associated Press / Álex Zea / Europa Press 85, Peter Barritt 59t, Stuart Black 76, blickwinkel / AGAMI / M. van Dijl 43b, Ian Canham 74t, Michelle Chaplow 78b, Classic Image 12cra, 56b, classicpaintings 58, Clearview 31b, Craig Jack Photographic 51, 94, Luis Dafos 126, dpa picture alliance 45br, Ilja Dubovskis 103b, Florapix 45cb, funkyfood London - Paul Williams 9cr, Gacro74 30b, Gaertner 15cr, Mario Galati 41t, Urs Hauenstein 6-7, Leroy Francis / Hemis.fr 33b, Heritage Image Partnership Ltd / Index 9tr, Image Professionals GmbH / LOOK-foto 27t, 39crb, 40, 68b, 92, imageBROKER / Diego Lezama 132, imageBROKER / Mara Brandl 21t, 72-73, imageBROKER / Unai Huizi 110t, imageBROKER.com / Egon Bömsch 41b, imageBROKER.com / Martin Jung 27b, imageBROKER.com / Moritz Wolf 25b, Japhotos 102, Jon Arnold Images Ltd / Alan Copson 29cra, Lanmas 8b, Gerg Lázár 21c, Little valleys 116, Jose Lucas 77, Stefano Politi Markovina 29tr, mauritius images GmbH 24, Tim Moore 134, Juan Carlos Muñoz 34bl, Perry van Munster 10bl, 80, 105, 117, myLAM 135, Old Books Images 8cla, Photo12 / Ann Ronan Picture Library 10tr, QEDimages 59b, M Ramírez 66, 82, Stefano Ravera 54, Realy Easy Star / Tullio Valente 35, Simon Reddy 12br, robertharding / Carlo Morucchio 97, robertharding / Neil Farrin 1, Felipe Rodriguez 95, Peter Schickert 13cl, 23t, Witold Skrypczak 48b, Maria Galan Still 78t, Stuart972-HDR 75t, Sueddeutsche Zeitung Photo 10cla, travelstock44.de / Juergen Held 96, Ivan Vdovin 91, Bax Walker 115, Ken Welsh 113, Werner Forman Archive / National Maritime Museum,Greenwich / Heritage Images 53, WINEOGRAPHIC 81t, Wim Wiskerke 32-33t, Wiskerke 56t, Sergi Reboredo / ZUMA Press Wire 13clb, ZUMA Press, Inc 84

AWL Images: Mauricio Abreu 11, 64-65b, 87, Jon Arnold 19, 36-37b, Davide Camesasca 37t, ImageBROKER 13cl (8), 70-71, J.Banks 38-39t,